SUMMON UP THE BLOOD

SUMMON UP THE BLOOD

A UNIQUE RECORD OF
D-DAY AND ITS AFTERMATH
by
Corporal J. A. WOMACK R. E.
edited by his daughter
CELIA WOLFE

In peace there's nothing so becomes a man
As modest stillness and humility:
But when the blast of war blows in our ears,
Then imitate the action of the tiger;
Stiffen the sinews, summon up the blood.

Henry V, Act III, Scene I

LEO COOPER
LONDON

First published in Great Britain in 1997 by
LEO COOPER
an imprint of
Pen & Sword Books Ltd
47 Church Street, Barnsley, South Yorkshire, S70 2AS

A CIP catalogue record for this book is available
from the British Library

ISBN 0 85052 537 3

Printed by Redwood Books Ltd,
Trowbridge, Wiltshire

Table of Contents

To the memory of my parents

Preface

It has long been my ambition to have my late father's war diary published. As a serious student of history, I have always thought that such a remarkable document should be shared, rather than gather dust on my bookshelves. My father was a corporal in the Royal Engineers and took part in the invasion of Normandy in June, 1944. For the rest of his life he was interested in anything to do with the invasion. As children we always marked the anniversary of D-Day. Even now 6 June never passes unnoticed.

I know that it was frowned upon for soldiers to keep diaries, but my father's was kept with the full cognizance of his Commanding Officer. As I understand it, he even encouraged him. My father was a history buff and, when he went on the invasion, was determined to keep as detailed a record as possible, knowing that his account would be of some interest in the future. He wrote up one, two, three or four days' accounts at a time, depending on the circumstances.

The diary opens on 28 May, 1944, somewhere near Southampton. My father mentions that he had been on the X list and already knew a good bit about the proposed landing. I know that he was involved in the planning from the Engineers' point of view. He had been picked out earlier in the war, had had his background investigated, been warned about the Official Secrets Act, and had spent time at Apsley House, London, where, he told us, he had to sleep in a bath because there was nowhere else! But it was enough for him to be living in the former residence of the Duke of Wellington, one of his heroes. He also spent a good bit of time near Largs in Western Scotland where they were testing landing craft and such like.

For the actual invasion he was attached to the 3rd Canadian Infantry Division. He landed at Bernières-sur-Mer on JUNO beach at H+3½ hours. He was part of Tac HQ of British 1st Corps and the immediate job was to establish communications between the 3rd Canadian and 3rd British Divisions.

The diary contains much technical information and details of the deployment of troops. Whatever his job was, he had access to information on a detailed scale. It is also a very human document, with touches of sadness, anger, frustration, but also humour. He comments on the effects of the war on the civilian population, and expresses his feelings for the enemy, which range from contempt to admiration and respect. He witnessed the battles for Caen, Falaise and the 'pocket', Le Havre and the push into Belgium. The diary finishes on 12 February, 1945, in Holland, (though my father went on into Germany and finished his war service at Iserlohn). On one occasion he was mentioned in despatches. He said it was for intercepting a crucial wireless message under bombardment. Unfortunately, although we have his bronze oak leaf, we are not in possession of a citation, so do not know the exact details.

My father's name was James Albert Womack. He was born in South Elmsall, West Yorkshire, on 21 May, 1916. He was born two months prematurely and was not expected to live. Apparently the midwife forced brandy between his lips to revive him – the taste for which he never lost! He also boasted that no one ever caught up the two-month start he had been given in life. A jab in the eye with the forceps at birth deprived him of the sight in his left eye. Ironically, he was later to depend for his living on the sight of his good eye – he became a professional photographer.

At the time of his birth the news was full of the town of Albert on the Ancre, where the build-up for the "Big Push" was based and, like many of his generation, he was named after the town. To distinguish him from an Uncle James who was serving at the Front with the King's Own Yorkshire Light Infantry, he was always known by his second Christian name.

He was lucky enough to win a scholarship to the Grammar School at Hemsworth and had six years of grammar school education. He had a particular flair for languages and was able to learn very quickly. I remember as a child how he was able to help me with my Latin homework, at a distance of about 35 years. When we visited the seaside, usually Scarborough, he would chat to the German or Dutch crewmen of the fishing boats in their own tongue with remarkable facility and he never lost his grasp of French.

However, like many boys of his day and background, a university education was out of the question. He could easily have tackled a science degree; his understanding of physics was particularly strong and I suspect that this was why he finished up in the Engineers. (His aptitude was not always applied in the right direction at school, however. On one occasion he secretly rigged up the school's Wimshurst machine in the boys' urinals and claimed to have thus sterilized some members of the First Eleven football team after an evening match.) His first love was history, which he read avidly, but in the end market forces propelled him into a commercial course at school – typing, shorthand and book-keeping. I think that he was destined for a 'safe' office-based career in his parents' eyes, but, apart from an involvement in insurance, he was not really the office type.

After the war and demobilization in 1946 my father returned to South Elmsall where he established a successful photography business, which is still in the family. He had married during the war to Mary Bowen of Kent. They had four children.

It was one of my father's dearest wishes to return to Normandy. He said that his foxholes were so well hidden that he would still be able to find them! Unfortunately, he developed heart disease in his forties, and the year that we were planning to take him back to Normandy, he died. That was 15 February, 1976. He was 59 years old. His two-month start had more than caught up with him.

My husband, son and I did eventually visit Normandy in the summer of 1985. I wanted to see the places he had spoken of so often for myself. We followed his diary from his landing beach through to Le Havre. It was a very moving experience, especially when we were able to link up with the Ledésert family in Caen, a family that my father had helped out after the terrible battle for that city. The paterfamilias was 99 years old, but his memory was still strong enough to remember Corporal Womack.

The diary has not been altered, simply punctuated where neces-sary. In his hurry to get things down on paper, abbreviations were used in the original. I decided to let some of these stand and give a glossary. I apologize for the use of terms such as "Jerry", "Boche", "Yanks" and "heluva", but they were common parlance at the time. My italicized introductions to the chapters are designed to put events into context as briefly as possible. I have investigated certain incidents in the diary, particularly where there is an element of controversy, and included notes and foot-notes in the chapters where appropriate. Some especially controversial claims, concerning the massacre of Canadian pris-oners of war and accidental bombing incidents, are dealt with separately in the Appendices. I have added my own observations, experiences and up-to-date photographs from my trips to Normandy.

So two journeys are interwoven here. My father's journey of more than fifty years ago takes precedence. My own travels were partly physical, but they also took me through various texts and Unit War Diaries, and along the way I met and corresponded with a number of veterans whose experiences overlapped with those of my father.

Although my father does try to give an overview at times, it must be remembered that the diary is written from one man's point of view and he puts down what was important to him. It may seem that some important details are neglected, but only because they did not impinge directly upon him. Also, occasional inaccuracies in his dates were found, but this is not really surprising under the circumstances. When he wrote up several days' entries at one go, the log-jam of memories would burst and I imagine that, in his haste and exhaustion, dates and locations would not always be exact. Curiously, the misconceptions arising out of the chaos of war, and his prejudices, are of value, for they show the feelings and beliefs (not always accurate) of soldiers at that time. Hindsight, of course, makes evaluation so much easier for us. But for the most part, his words are supported by the Unit War Diaries, among other sources, and in the main, I was more heartened than frustrated in my research!

I felt very close to my father during the months of research. At times I have almost sensed him standing at my shoulder, urging me on. He has been dead for twenty years, but it has been like renewing a friendship.

Celia Wolfe
September, 1996

Acknowledgements

I would like to extend my sincere thanks to all who have helped me in the preparation of this book. One of the most satisfying aspects of my research was the opportunity to meet and correspond with so many helpful people.

I would like to pay special thanks to Roy Cullingworth (ex-R.E. British 1st Corps) who helped to check details in the diary, to Walter Horne (Duke of Wellington's Regiment) for allowing me access to his written and photographic records, and to the following veterans who kindly allowed me to use their memories: Jack Armitage (7th Btn. Duke of Wellington's Regt.), G.M. Baxter (Air Observation Post), D. Blackburn (18th Armoured Car Regt.), P.J. Carter (Royal Canadian Engineers), H.C. Chadderton (Royal Winnipeg Rifles), C.A. Clemens (Royal Canadian Artillery), H. Danter (R.C.A.), J.V. Derych (Polish Artillery), James Dunphy (52 Lowland Division), R.G. Haine (R.C.A.), Harvey Hill (R.C.A.), Walter Horne (Duke of Wellington's Regt.), W.S. Stonewall Jackson (R.C.A.), James Johnston (4 Canadian Armoured Division), R. Langdale (Hallamshire Btn.) D.A. Moss (R.C.A.), J. O'Neill (Royal Engineers), James Nightingale (52 (L) Div.), Dixon Raymond (3rd Canadian Infantry Division), L. Robertson (South Saskatchewan Regt.), S.D. Robinson (Royal Signals), Graham Roe (Hallamshire Btn.), Fred Rogers (R.C.A.), Frank Rowlands (Pioneer Corps), Lloyd Taylor (21 Field Dressing Station) and Joseph Wagar (Queen's Own Rifles of Canada).

My thanks are due to the staff of the P.R.O., the Royal Engineers Museum, the Brotherton Library, Leeds University, to Don Scott, Keeper (Militaria) York and Lancaster Regimental Museum, and Stephen Campbell at the National Archives of Canada for their assistance during my research. Special thanks go to Peter Liddle of Leeds University for his advice and encouragement.

I would like to acknowledge all the kind assistance and hospitality that I received on my visits to Normandy, especially from the staff of the library and archives at the Museum for Peace, Caen, M. Georges Bernage of Editions Heimdal, Bayeux, Mme. Monique Corblet de Fallerans, M. and Mme. Daniel Ledésert, M.J. Guillot, the proprietors of the Château d'Audrieu, and the Keeper of the Flak Tower Museum, Ouistreham.

I owe a debt of gratitude to the Goldsmiths' Company of London who awarded me a Travelling Grant for Teachers in the summer term of 1995, permitting me to pursue my research in London and Normandy without distractions, while my teaching and responsibilities were being taken care of. Special thanks go to my colleague Lorna Warren.

I am also grateful for permission to use quotations from the following: *Maple Leaf Route: Falaise*, by T. Copp and R. Vogel; *The Army Air Forces in World War II: Vol. 3*, by W.F. Craven and J.L. Cate; *With the 6th Airborne Division in Normandy*, by Lt. Gen. R.N. Gale; *Normandy to Arnhem*, by Brig. T. Hart Dyke; *Caen: Anvil of Victory*, by A. McKee; *The History of the Corps of Royal Engineers, Vol. IX*, by Maj. Gen. R.P. Packenham-Walsh; *Le Geste du Régiment de la Chaudière*, by Majors A. Ross and M. Gauvin; *1944: The Canadians in Normandy*, by R. Roy; *The History of the 51st Highland Division, 1939–1945*, by J.B. Salmond; *The Canadian Army, 1939–1945*, by C.P. Stacey; and from the Unit War Diaries in the P.R.O. Crown copyright material in the P.R.O. is reproduced by permission of the Controller of Her Majesty's Stationery Office.

I thank my brother John Womack for helping me with the photographs; and Elizabeth Grew, Alan Rothwell and Marlies Dufour for helping me with my translations.

In closing, I offer a very special thanks for the patience, understanding and encouragement of my husband, Raymond, and son, James, during the preparation of this book.

C.W.

Glossary

The most common military words are officially abbreviated, for instance, 'Division' was always 'Div', 'Infantry' was 'Inf', 'Artillery' became 'Arty', Company was 'Coy', etc.

AA	Anti-Aircraft Artillery
ADC	Aide-de-Camp
AFV	Armoured Fighting Vehicle
AG	Adjutant General
AGRA	Army Group, Royal Artillery
APO	Army Post Office
ARMD	Armoured
ASLT	Assault
AVRE	Armoured Vehicle, Royal Engineers
AUSTER	A 100 m.p.h. single-engined plane of the Air Observation Post, from which artillery fire could be directed.
BANGALORE	Torpedo tube full of explosive
BEAD	To have in one's sights (from the sighting projection at the end of a gun barrel)
BEEHIVE	75 lbs of explosive standing on 3 stems, carried by 2 men, and placed on top of the target. The blast went downwards and could penetrate 12 feet of concrete.
BGS	Brigadier, General Staff
BOCAGE	Hedgerow countryside
CCRA	Commander Corps Royal Artillery
CCS	Casualty Clearing Station or Combined Chiefs of Staff
CE	Chief Engineer
CHESPALE	Chestnut palings used in bundles as fascines
CRAB	Usually a Sherman tank with an extended pair of arms carrying a flail to clear minefields
CRE	Commander, Royal Engineers
CROCODILE	Churchill tank modified as a flamethrower
DA & QMG	Deputy Adjutant & Quartermaster General
DAG	Deputy Adjutant General
DD	Duplex Drive (amphibious)

DF-ING	Direction Finding.
DR	Dispatch Rider
DUKW	Dual drive 2½ ton amphibious truck
E-BOAT	German naval attack boat
FBE	Folding Boat Equipment
FD PK COY RE	Field Park Company Royal Engineers
FFI	*Forces Françaises de l'Intérieur* – the Resistance
GAF	German Air Force
I	Intelligence
KANGAROO	De-gunned carrier in which 10 fully equipped infantrymen could be packed
KL	A member of the Kempisch Legioen, a resistance group based in de Kempen, a region of Antwerp.
L OF C	Lines of Communication
LCG	Landing Craft, Gun
LCA	Landing Craft, Assault – carried 35 troops
LCI	Landing Craft, Infantry – carried 200 troops or 75 tons of cargo
LCS	Landing Craft, Support
LCT	Landing Craft, Tank – carried 4 tanks
LST	Landing Ship, Tank – carried 1,600 to 1,900 tons of vehicles or cargo
MTB	Motor Torpedo Boat
PETARD	An AVRE on a Churchill chassis with a short barrelled mortar which fired a 40 lb 'flying dustbin' – an explosive charge used to destroy pillboxes and other obstructions
PIAT	Projector, Infantry, Anti-Tank – a light infantry anti-tank weapon
RA	Royal Artillery
SBG	Small Box Girder – a type of bridge
SITREP	Situation Report produced at 24-hour intervals
SO	Signals Officer
SP	Self-Propelled
TAC	Advanced Tactical H.Q.
TELLERMINE	German anti-vehicle mine
TPS	Troops
VIC	An abbreviation of Victor, the 'call sign' on the radio in the HQ wireless truck.
WASP	A universal carrier with flamethrower and 80 gallon tank of jellied petroleum. Carried a 3-man crew.
X LIST	Personnel involved in the planning of Operation Overlord.

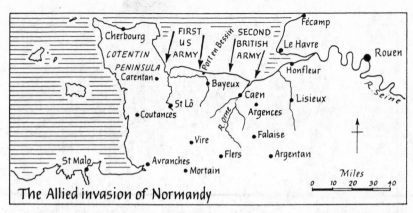

The Allied invasion of Normandy

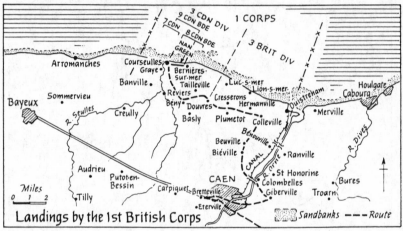

Landings by the 1st British Corps

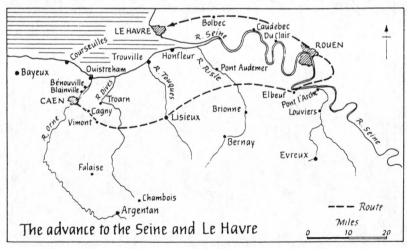

The advance to the Seine and Le Havre

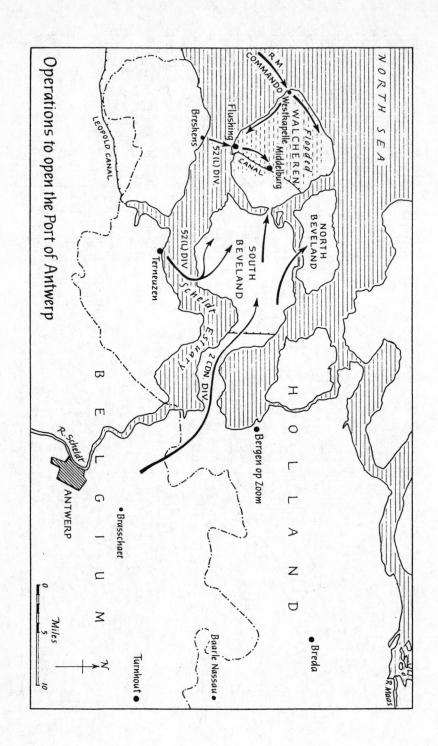

Operations to open the Port of Antwerp

Chapter One

The Beaches

The Allied invasion of France by British, Canadian and American forces took place on 6 June, 1944, along a fifty-mile front stretching from the mouth of the River Orne in the east to the base of the Cotentin Peninsula in the west. The front was divided into five beaches code-named OMAHA and UTAH (American), JUNO (Canadian) and GOLD and SWORD (British). The plan for the British and Canadians was to form an initial beachhead ten miles deep with the city of Caen as the first-day objective. They then had to pin down ten Panzer divisions at Caen to allow the Americans to make the decisive break-through at the other end of the beachhead. Unfortunately an advance of six miles instead of ten on that first day meant that the city did not fall for another six weeks, and in that time it was reduced to a grave-yard for soldiers and citizens alike.

The immediate task on 6 June was to land near low water on a rising tide to allow time for the demolition of German beach obstacles. This would permit the landing craft to disembark, retire on a rising tide and go back for the next load. (On high water and a falling tide the craft would lie helplessly as targets for enemy guns.) But it is well known that adverse weather conditions affected these plans. A Force 5 wind from the south-west (19–24 m.p.h. on the Beaufort Scale) whipped up the sea and many troops were sea-sick. An unexpectedly high tide due to the gale wrecked landing craft on the beach obstacles and so restricted the movement of vehicles on the beaches. The weather also put the launching of DD tanks in jeopardy. In the end some were not launched (but beached later), some were swamped on launching and sank with their crews (as at Omaha), and some were launched success-fully. Because of the weather the air bombardment largely missed the beach defences, the bombs falling well inland.

A determined German defence did put a brake on the dash forward.

1

Towns like Courseulles and Bernières rapidly became choked with troops and vehicles, and tanks were having difficulty in getting off beaches which were becoming steadily narrower as the tide rose. This congestion on the beaches meant that there was a delay in pushing through fresh assault troops who were to make the dash inland.

To balance these disadvantages, it has to be said that if the weather had been kinder the Germans might have acted more decisively and sooner than they did. As it was, Rommel and other senior commanders were absent from their posts, on leave or on exercise. The two nearest available divisions were Witt's 12th SS Panzer Grenadier Division (Hitler Youth), thirty miles south of Lisieux, and Bayerlein's Panzer Lehr Division, 75 miles south-west of Paris. They could only be moved on Hitler's orders, but, as has been well chronicled, Hitler was in a drugged sleep on the morning of 6 June, from which no one dared wake him. D-Day was more than half over before Hitler finally awoke, by which time this available armour had to move without early morning mist cover and under air attack.

This left only the 21st Panzer Division (with about 120 tanks) near enough to the landing area to counter-attack on D-Day itself. They were established around Caen while the West Wall defences were in the hands of the 716th Infantry Division. The 21st Panzers faced Crocker's British 1st Corps, whose immediate task was to take Caen and the high ground of the Falaise road to the south of the city. While the 6th Airborne Division cleared and held the left flank, the 3rd Canadian Infantry Division and 2nd Canadian Armoured Brigade were to cover the right flank by cutting the Caen–Bayeux road from Putot-en-Bessin to Carpiquet, to allow the main thrust to be made on the city by the 3rd British Infantry Division with 27th Armoured Brigade.

At the end of the first day, while British newspapers were reporting street fighting in Caen, German counter-attacks had been made, but delayed, both by Hitler and the actions of the RAF, and the British advance had been slowed, with tanks getting forward without infantry and vice versa. During the weeks that followed the enemy deployed his best formations against the invader and kept the Allied armies contained in Normandy. As reinforcements and supplies poured ashore, the invasion turned into a war of attrition with some of the most costly and vicious fighting of the North West Campaign. Only gradually, as the sheer weight of men, armour and air superiority on the Allied side began to tell, did the tide begin to turn in favour of the Allies.

Sunday 28 May
It is now farewell to Cobham for at long last the War Lords have decided to 'have a go' and today, loaded down with everything we possess, we are shepherded into a Concentration Area somewhere near Southampton. We are housed under canvas, but the weather is good so this doesn't matter. Also we are issued with camp beds and we are not losing any time getting into them. It has been a hard journey in the troop carrier.

Monday 29 May
This camp is a very big one and hidden away in a wood and is housing the D Day boys to be, or at least some of them; I have seen members of the 3 Br Div and 3Cdn also. I will be going with the Cdns although I prefer to be with the British. I see there are a number of French Cdns here, Régiment de la Chaudière and North Shore. These fellows think that it is another exercise. I would love to disillusion them, but they might 'beat it' if they knew what they were in for. It would be very difficult to get out of this place for it is heavily guarded and surrounded by barbed wire. No civilians are allowed here and I doubt if our letters will be posted until after D Day.

Tuesday 30 May
We have absolutely no work whatsoever to do. We just lounge around in the sun, sleep and eat and visit the three camp cinemas; basketball games are organised and scratch concerts. The NAAFI has a good stock of bad beer, and we drink quite a lot of it too. A little excitement was caused today by the issuing of French francs.

Wednesday 31 May
We were today 'briefed' by Brig Balfour, BGS (*Brigadier, General Staff*) 1 Corps. He did not disclose the place where we are to land, but chiefly told us what to do on landing so that we wouldn't appear like a lot of waifs and strays; each man was issued with a Disembarkation Card and in the event of him getting lost he is to report to an Assembly Area, named 'Frankie' and, armed with the card, will be told where to go. All this was quite a waste to myself and friends as we could have told them this information last March, including the landing place. We are constantly being asked by the others where we are going, for it is known that we were on the X List.

3

Thursday 1 June

The good weather is still holding out and I am feeling a little impatient to get started. We are still lolling around, eating excellent food, playing cards for francs and speculating on what will happen on D Day. The rest has done me a world of good and I feel very fit. I write every day to Mary but she won't get these letters for some time yet. Poor Mary, she expects me back in Shamley tomorrow – thinks I am on a week's exercise. What will she think when she reads of the Invasion on D Day? I'm so pleased she doesn't know.

Friday 2 June

Now we are getting somewhere. Today we were transported to Southampton docks and embarked on our respective craft. I was so pleased to see that my ship carried the name *The Duke of Wellington*. I couldn't invade under a better title. The *D.W.* is a large ship of some 15,000 tons and very modern. She carries 6 light Assault Landing Craft, for her passengers are in the first and second waves. We are a little crowded in our quarters below decks and ventilation is poor. The hammocks which we sleep in, though, are fairly comfortable and many a laugh is caused as a chap unexpectedly rolls out.

Saturday 3 June

There seems to be something severely wrong with the water on this ship for the tea has a taste as of creosote. It is very interesting now as we anchor off the Isle of Wight and watch all the different ships jockeying for position. I know some of the types, but it appears that the Navy has a few 'secret weapons' too; today I had a good view of a rocket ship – a surprise packet for the French coast.

Sunday 4 June

There appears to be a change in the weather coming for the sea is quite rough and we have had a little rain. The chaps are getting restless and are itching to get going. We had to go back into Southampton today for fresh water – there *is* creosote in this water. The water tanks had not properly dried after being creosoted. Well anyway we can't grumble at the Navy. They gave us a double rum issue to make up for it.

4

Monday 5 June

This morning I sensed that today we would sail, for all the ships seemed beautifully in position. Also the Minesweepers had set out to the head of the convoy. There were the huge LCTs with their decks covered with vehicles, LCIs, containing men of the two finest Divisions in the world, Assault Craft, Rocket Ships, Cross Channel Steamers, Destroyers, Cruisers, MTBs, LCAs, LSIs, even RAF launches.* When this convoy is added to the one departing Tilbury there will be a total of 4,000 ships. Later this afternoon Mr Churchill and Gen Smuts cruised round the convoy, Churchill giving his famous V sign. After that the naval personnel were briefed, for so far they were not in the 'know' and were under the impression that this was just another exercise. They were told that we would sail at 2100 hrs – we were going in – and that there would be no coming back or retiring. The weather was now very bad and many of the chaps were ill; our French Cdn friends were very seasick, and also very excited. 2100 hrs we were off. This is it. My thoughts are very mixed. In some respects I am pleased that the Invasion has at last occurred for this awful war must end. I felt a little anxious for Mary. She would be very worried when she heard of our attack. I wonder what she would do if anything happened to me, but of course nothing will happen to me. The Padre, though, in his prayer said that some of we chaps were cheerfully giving our lives to make a better world, that we were Crusaders and a lot more that made the majority of us feel miserable. I had a good go at the rum and that put me in a better mood. A lousy S/Sgt in the RA had the jitters. He stopped us from dozing by telling us all about the terrific defences there were on the Great West Wall. I know where every one of those defences are. He doesn't know on which part of the coast we are landing yet. Capt Knight came round at about 2200 hrs and told our little party that they would be forming Tactical HQ of 1 Corps and that our job was to establish communications to the two divs as quickly as possible after the initial assault. We were to land between Bernières-sur-Mer and Courseulles on Nan/Green beach on the second flight about H + 3½. Nobody slept tonight. We all sat and listened to the wind and rain which had now risen to almost gale force. Vomit bags were very well used. I never felt the least bit sick. My chief reactions were anxiety for Mary and mother and

* Landing Craft, Tank; Landing Craft, Infantry; Motor Torpedo Boat; Landing Craft, Assault; Landing Ship, Infantry.

father. They were sure to worry, although I had repeatedly told them not to worry about me as I could more than look after myself. If the secret of the Invasion has not leaked out then we will walk it. The 3 Br and 3 Cdn on our sector are the finest shock troops in the world – WHEN THEY GET THEIR FEET ON SOLID GROUND – we can just hope. I went on deck about 0200 hrs. It was pitch black, we were moving fairly quickly. I couldn't see the other boats, but I knew they were there. Somewhere in this huge convoy is Frank. I wondered where he will be landing. It's a bit rough on Frank. This is his second trip out here. He's getting on a bit too to be participating in such an escapade. I hope he'll be alright.* I noticed little buoys with lights every ½ mile or so. They were put there by the minesweepers who had to clear a lane across the English Channel. I felt very proud of our Navy. They are a marvellous organisation; no flap or panic as they transport this huge army to Normandy. The *DW* stopped and began to roll horribly in the huge swell. When dawn broke I could see the dim outline of the coast.

Tuesday 6 June

As the *DW* rolled about and the light got better we could make out the dim coastline of Normandy. It was 0530 hrs. All about us were hundreds of ships of all shapes and sizes. I wondered why the coastal guns at Houlgate, Cabourg, Lion-sur-Mer and Courseulles didn't open up on us. A Navy officer showed me the answer in ten beautiful cruisers all in a row waiting for these guns to give their positions away. H hour was to be at 0745 hrs but could be adjusted by the admiral in charge, *not* Montgomery's representative, for the Navy are the Senior Service and i/c landing operations on operation Overlord.† We looked at our equipment a thousand times and carefully checked our weapons. We tested and re-tested our Mae Wests and we stood and watched and waited. Then it came. 500 Fortresses dropped 900 tons of bombs between Bernières and Courseulles, swarms of fighters machine-gunned the defences, the rocket ships rained their missiles on the beaches by the thousand and the *Rodney* and the *Warspite* rolled

* My father's older brother. A volunteer in his early 40's in the Royal Army Service Corps, he had been on the Norway expedition (1940) and the evacuation from Dunkirk. He had joined up when my father received his call-up papers to give his younger brother moral support.
† Some Army officers found that they had to obey orders from Naval officers, junior to them in rank, during landing operations.

up and gave those defences hell in the form of 18" shells weighing one ton each. The din was terrific. I never thought that mere man could make such a noise, it was terrifying to hear at times. The big ships began to lower their assault craft and so our first flight got ready; they also were lowered down the side. Crouching in the bottom of their craft they looked very tiny and when they were afloat, they rocked and rolled so much that I thought they would capsize. We gave them a cheer as the six boats roared away. They were grand fellows those Chaudières. I wondered how many would make the grade. By this time the bombardment had ceased. It would take the assault craft about an hour to run in. They had good air support from Spits and Mustangs of 84 Group RAF. The coastline was well ablaze by this time. Occasional explosions suggested that the Assault Engineers of 5th Assault RE were at work on the beach obstacles. Underwater obstacles had to be removed, mines and barbed wire to be dealt with, but the biggest job these boys had was to blow a gap in the sea wall to let the tanks get off the beach. We waited for our turn to come but the boats seemed to be late in returning. There was all hell let loose ashore now. Somebody out there was making history. A couple of German 190s attacked but came down almost before they set off. 30 Corps were on our right; they were going in with 50 Div and 7 Armd with 49 Div in reserve. Our 6 Airborne Div would by this time have gained most of their objectives for they touched down at 0100 hrs this morning. I wondered whether Rex was in 6 Airborne.* At last one of our assault craft returned to tell us the bad news that the other five craft had capsized after landing their cargo, on the return journey.† Immediately a LCI drew alongside and we had rather a bad job jumping from the *DW* to this other craft as the two ships swung one way and then the other. It was a most dangerous operation and two men failed to make it. There were a few dead Cdns aboard this ship and also a few shell-shocked or bomb-happy men – they came back laughing – but the naval personnel told us that all was going well. We headed for the beach and as I peeped over the side I could see Bernières was a blazing inferno. The second flight got under was as other craft joined us. As we drew near I could hear the crackle of small arms

* Lt Rex Gladwin, my father's best friend from school days, landed at Ranville with 6 Airborne.
† This sounds bad but losses overall were not as high as feared. Ninety of the 306 landing craft on the Canadian beaches were lost or damaged.

fire and the chatter of machine guns; mines were exploding too. It must have been about four miles to the beach and I don't think our particular craft was actually the target of a German gun during the whole run in. We passed two LCIs lying on their sides in the shallow water. We were very close now. We were ordered to keep low and prepare to land. Those last few minutes were agonising. I expected any time to be blown clean out of the water either by a Tellermine placed on a pole under the water or by one of the coastal guns. But no, the flat-bottomed craft grated to a standstill, the doors were opened and there, 200 yds ahead, were the beaches. We poured out of the craft as quickly as we could and waded ashore. A hundred isolated pictures fill the mind of the man who is taking part in the great assault. They have little sequence or connection. There is no grand comprehensive view, but each one is burned into his mind for life. I was so very excited at the time that I'm not quite sure what I did see. I looked at a few horrible sights without seeing them. I had never seen many dead men before and I often wondered how I should react. They just didn't register. The Chaudières had done remarkably well and had driven the Huns out of Bernières when we arrived except for a few snipers who were still being winkled out. The 5th Assault RE had blown two beautiful gaps in the sea-wall in this sector and thus the tanks were able to get inland very quickly. There was no doubt that the 716 (German) Inf Div had been caught napping. Already prisoners were beginning to assemble on the beaches – and made to work too. They were carrying off the dead. In file and very much alert we proceeded to Bernières. Our packs were exceedingly heavy for they contained everything we would need for the next 3 days. We passed a German pillbox. It was a horrible twisted wreck and two machine-gunners were in the same condition. As we approached the village it didn't seem to be on fire as badly as we first thought. The villagers looking very much afraid, stood timidly watching us. We gave them cigarettes and chocolate. They had gone through a far tougher time than we had and I felt very sorry for an old lady who was badly wounded. The RAMC [Royal Army Medical Corps] were giving her first aid. We made for a huge château and settled down to prepare a meal from our 24-hour ration pack. I approached the house which was about finished; it was empty. It had been on fire. I was wanting water if possible to cook some porridge. I wandered round the place and found a trench in the garden and there I saw a middle-aged lady all crumpled up. I told her that she could come out and

8

that the Germans had gone. She looked deathly pale as I assisted her, but as she looked at her house she was very brave. I said, '*Avez vous du l'eau, Madame, s'il vous plaît?*' In perfect English she replied, 'There should be a well round the other side of the house'. She then told me that in the ruins somewhere was her husband. A long burst of machine-gun fire sent her scurrying back to the trench. I got the water and fed well.*

We then started off to Courseulles which was our D Day objective. We were very elated at our easy landing. It felt good to get our feet on terra firma again. We could operate now. We were helpless whilst on the sea. Some of the chaps broke into song and our packs felt light. I must get news to Mary and mother that I am OK; I wonder when that will be possible. These were my main thoughts. I knew I wouldn't get killed. Our party hadn't even a casualty. I felt as though the war was over, until a shell fell uncomfortably close and we all had to 'bite the dust'. Anyway I was at least on land. I felt very, very good. Hundreds of thousands of troops would be pouring ashore during the next few days. We'd made it. On arriving at Courseulles we took our first German prisoner. He said he had deserted and was actually a Russian, captured at Smolensk and forced to fight for the Germans – he never wanted to fight anyway (?) This village had received a heluva pounding and the occupants were badly shaken. Three dead cows blocked our path but they hadn't stopped a tank from forcing its way forward. On arriving at our particular orchard we were told to immediately dig in as a German counter-attack was expected that night. I dug five different slit trenches in five different places for every time I settled in I was wanted to guard a different position. This Normandy earth is mighty tough too. Every field had the same warning posts in German 'Achtung Minen', but every field hadn't got mines in them. A dummy mine-field can prove a very delaying obstacle though for they all have to be swept. At last we are all nicely dug in for the night. Brig Longden, DA & QMG [Deputy Adjutant and Quartermaster General] 1 Corps visits us in turn. He is in very good spirits and predicts an early finish to the war. He points out a wood about a mile away where a party of Germans are still holding out and we have called on the RAF to do a bit of straffing. At 2100 hrs the

---

* The first 'native' he spoke to was English! She came from Clapham and had married a Frenchman. In fact my father tidied up the story for his diary. The lady was not quite so polite in her response.

9

fighter bombers came in very low and gave that wood all they had for about 15 minutes. I would have thought that nothing could have possibly lived in there, but inside ½ hr after the planes departed we came under shell fire from that very same wood. We now seemed to hold but a few fields and as we sat in our slit trenches we wondered what the night was to be like. We had obviously caught Jerry on one leg during the landing and got a foothold very cheaply indeed. It all remained to see how quickly Jerry could get reorganised for a counter-offensive. As darkness came on the first wave of German bombers came in. Our AA was supplied by the Navy and they threw up everything they had including the 'kitchen stove'. Jerry just couldn't miss a target no matter where he dropped his bombs for we were getting very packed in our small bridgehead. Sgt Foubister and I crouched in the bottom of the trench and never has a trench seemed so shallow and so wide as that one did. We were straffed and bombed all night, petrol dumps blew up and ships were hit, vehicles were set on fire and Bernières and Courseulles were subjected once more to another bombardment. One bomb fell extra close and momentarily I was stunned by the concussion; my left ear seized up on me too.

In notes that my father wrote on the 30th Anniversary of D Day, he added a few more details to his original diary entry. He wrote: "We transferred to an LCI about four miles out. We took along with us 50 Royal Engineers of the Airborne Division complete with folding bicycles. They were to get ashore as quickly as possible and cycle to Ranville to join their comrades who had airdropped the night before. As our LCI ground to a halt opposite Bernières-sur-Mer, we came under light fire, and met our first obstacle – the 50 bikes laid in the doorway of the LCI! It was chaos – ammo boots and spokes, handlebars, pedals, brakes. We crashed over the lot and into the water about waist deep . . . My outstanding recollection was the incredible din . . . Rocket ships and barges with artillery all belting away. Low-flying fighter bombers machine-gunning enemy emplacements. Tank engines roaring and flails beating the sand. Tanks on fire, tanks exploding, mines exploding, men shouting. We ran and ran. First it was hard sand, then soft sand but we never slowed down." (Father, who had sprinted in athletics meetings for the Royal Engineers, ran to the sea wall to take cover. As he bounced off the wall, one of his officers commented, "We're going to blow this sea wall down, Womack, not knock it down!")

10

"We were ashore. What a relief. We had had an easy landing. The underwater obstacles weren't underwater because we landed at low tide. These were plain to see and consisted of three pieces of railway line about four feet high crossing each other with a tellermine on the top. These were smashed by the flail tanks. The beach mines were also flailed, the small beach wall was breached by Petard tanks which fired a 'flying dustbin'. We carried a 'Beehive', called this because of its shape. It is fastened to the beach wall and when fired blows a gap 16 feet wide at an angle of less than 45 degrees. We never had to use it.

"Next to Courseulles, this time mine-lifting. The Germans had signed their minefields with a board on which was drawn a skull and crossbones and the words 'Achtung Minen'. But not all were mine-fields. Some were dummy minefields where they had sown any pieces of metal that would register on our Polish mine detectors. But all had to be moved that lay in our path. We put white tapes 16 feet apart through these minefields as they were lifted. Many of the mines were useless. They had been in this marshy land so long, they had rusted. But we dare not take chances. Finally to Courseulles. The first prisoner was a Russian! He pointed his empty rifle to the sky to tell us he had never fired on the British – always above."

My father landed on the extreme left of Nan/Green beach at Bernières-sur-Mer. The Chaudières were on the extreme right of Nan/White, as reserve to the Queen's Own Rifles of Canada. The first objective of the Regina Rifles on Nan/Green beach was Courseulles, which may explain why his first task was to make his way here, one mile from neighbouring Bernières. He therefore witnessed the scenes on two landing beaches.

The War Diary of the 8th Canadian Infantry Brigade gives a graphic description of the landings at Bernières: "0630 D Day. Sighted Bernières and St Aubin. The landmarks which had been carefully memorized from air photographs were clearly recognizable – the jetty at the harbour of Courseulles – the flat expanse of marshland to the east – then the church steeple amid a profusion of trees, which marked Bernières and on down the coast to the cluster of buildings surrounding the next church which marked St Aubin-sur-Mer. As the coast drew nearer the wind increased and a heavy sea made it necessary to consider whether or not the DD (Duplex Drive) tanks were to be launched.

"0700 Visibility lessening. The expectant and eager troops of the assault companies loaded into their LCAs. The armada slowly approached the shore and at 0725 LCGs opened fire on beach defences.

"0745 Bernières and St Aubin receiving terrific pounding though the

11

main effect seemed to be more inland and not on the immediate beach defences.

"0749 The rocket ships manoeuvred into position and fired their salvoes, but owing to poor visibility and smoke the effect was not observed. A few moments later word was received that the assault companies were ready for the dash to the shore.

"0810 During the run in very little opposition was evident. No enemy aircraft appeared and a small number of our own aircraft showed up during this time. At approximately 0812 AVREs (Armoured Vehicle, Royal Engineers) were seen touching down on beach, closely followed by assault companies." (WO 179/2886, 6 June, 1944)

Four companies of the Regina Rifles landed on Nan/Green between 8.05 a.m. and 8.55 a.m. Air support had not been as good as expected due to the adverse weather, so pillboxes and other emplacements were still open for business when the troops touched down. The Chaudières landed at Bernières from 8.30 onwards, encountering great difficulties with beach obstacles. For instance, only one of the five landing craft of A Company reached the beach undamaged.

Because of the weather conditions, the landings in the Canadian sector were delayed by about 35 minutes and this, combined with an abnormally high tide, meant that the beach obstacles were so deeply submerged that effective clearance had to wait until the tide turned. The report of the Canadian Field Companies R.C.E. (Royal Canadian Engineers) on Nan/Green beach highlights some of the difficulties the engineers faced. "Two sections under Lt Madge experienced some difficulty in landing due to the high water. Three mines on obstacles detonated under one craft with no casualties but damaging the ramp ... Ropes were rigged behind the D7s (bulldozers) and the men were towed ashore through the rough water and spasmodic enemy small arms fire. The height of water prevented any successful removal of obstacles by towing and several attempts to rig the demolition charges failed and finally had to be abandoned, as it became apparent that obstacle removal would have to be carried out on the falling tide. The time was utilised in breaking down the groynes which were blocking lateral communications on the beach. The falling tide revealed a very dense pattern of obstacles each of which had some type of mine attached. Most were wired with 75mm shells . . .; others had Tellermines wired on. Sections were organised in removing mines and obstacles. Occasional mortar fire interfered with the work on this beach but did not prevent the work proceeding faster than the falling tide so that the men were working in deep water most of the time. 450 yards were eventually removed." (War Diary Commander Royal Engineers 3rd Canadian Infantry Division WO179/2775, 6 June, 1944)

Some time later Canadian Intelligence revealed that the underwater obstacles had been troublesome, but not always very effective. Though tellermines had holed a number of craft, the mining of the obstacles had been incomplete and not all the obstacles were in position on D Day. "A point of minor interest is that objects previously thought to be shells fitted with detonators on the top of stakes turned out to be large bottles filled with explosive." (War Diary Canadian First Army General Staff (Intelligence) WO 179/2605, 15 June, 1944)

The 5th Assault Regiment R.E. had the task of putting the armour ashore ahead of the infantry on this sector of Juno beach. Each squadron of the regiment was split into two teams, one to deal with beach and underwater obstacles, the other to achieve the gapping of the main beach exits. The gapping team on Nan/Green was 80th Squadron. The anti-tank ditch was filled with fascines dropped by AVREs, armoured bulldozers improved the lanes between the mines, and the team used petards to blow gaps in the sea wall and to destroy steel obstacles in the beach exits. Both beach exits were working by about 9.00 a.m. At Bernières one exit was blown through the high sea wall and at another point, a small box girder assault bridge was placed over the wall by an AVRE. The cost of dealing with these obstacles to the 5th and 6th Assault Regiments R.E. was high with 25 killed, 63 wounded and 54 missing, probably drowned. But without their sacrifice, losses to other units trapped on the beaches would have been much higher.

Once the exits were cleared, the assault troops were able to move inland. The 1st Battalion The Queen's Own Rifles of Canada were off the beach at Bernières by 9.00 a.m. when, much to their surprise, "at this time it is noticed that a cafe just a hundred yards off the beach is opened up and selling wine to all and sundry." (War Diary WO 179/2958, 6, June 1944) The Régiment de la Chaudière came next. Largely French speakers, they were especially well received by the Normans. "The village of Bernières-sur-Mer is almost wholly destroyed and many of the houses are on fire. The French are fairly welcoming and many cheer us amongst the ruins of their homes." (War Diary WO 179/2941, 6 June, 1944)

In fact, the reception was mixed. In some instances, the welcome by Normans in the countryside was rather cool. The Germans had given little trouble to the country dwellers, for Normandy, being prosperous farming land, meant that the Germans did not wish to upset the

13

Normans. In fact, many Germans had married Norman girls and "lived off the fat of the land". This tranquillity had been upset by the invasion, when it was unavoidable that the inhabitants should suffer damage and casualties. In the towns it was different. Town dwellers had had a thin time and they welcomed their liberators with open arms.

The first prisoners of war were members of the 716 Infantry Division, a number of them Russians and according to the 13 Canadian Field Regiment R.C.A. (Royal Canadian Artillery): "All glad to be out of the war. The general impression of the prisoners being taken was their poor physique and no middle age group." (WO 179/3051, 6 June, 1944)

By the end of that first evening, the writer of the same War Diary reflected the experiences of most: "German air activity was apparent throughout the night . . . All ranks became eager and efficient in digging slit trenches . . . Fatigue was noticeable due to 24-hour packs, the rough voyage over, lack of sleep and the natural tension of a combined operation against a prepared enemy." The sentiments of the writer of the Diary of the Queen's Own Rifles of Canada must have been general: "The lads who fell on the beach itself were rather a disheartening sight – many of them trained for years and only lasted for a few moments in action. Many a good man was lost on these beaches but they did a wonderful job." (op. cit., 7 June, 1944)

Chapter Two

The Dash for Caen and the German Counter-Attacks

The plan was for the British to keep the Germans occupied at Caen for up to three weeks, to give the Americans time to break out of their bridgehead and swing the whole Allied line through an angle of ninety degrees, with Caen as the pivot. The German army would then be pushed back to the Seine, where it would be destroyed by tanks freed from the hindrance of the hedgerow countryside of the Normandy bocage. The Americans, however, were late to break out, partly because the storms of 20–23 June destroyed the American Mulberry harbour at Omaha and interrupted supplies. The Caen "hinge" became a cauldron that nearly broke the British, Canadian and German armies.

From D + 1 there was a steady build-up of Allied forces while Panzer Divisions, in the face of terrific RAF attacks, were poured into the Caen sector to mount an offensive that would push the British and Canadians back into the sea. The roads radiate out of Caen like the spokes of a wheel. While the Allies pushed down the spokes towards the hub, the Germans counter-attacked up them, and so a scene of confusion emerged as battles surged back and forth on the roads, rather like the tide. Meanwhile, a number of German strongpoints survived within Allied lines, like the Radar Station at Tailleville which was not captured until 17 June.

On 7 June a counter-attack by 12 SS Panzer Division and 21st Panzer Division, to throw the Allies back into the sea, was brought up short by a barrage of one-ton shells from the warships, leading to a temporary deadlock.

From 10 June there came a three-division attempt by the Germans to push the Allies back: by 21st Panzer Division from the East of

15

Caen, 12 SS from the centre and Panzer Lehr from the west of Caen and towards Bayeux. At the same time the Allied plan was for an encirclement of Caen to the east and west: the "left hook" in the east by 51 (H) Division from the Airborne bridgehead; the "right hook" in the west by 30 Corps and 7th Armoured Division from Bayeux towards Villers Bocage and Evrecy; and the 3rd Canadian Division was to advance between these two pincers a day or so later.

The head-on meetings of these two three-pronged attacks led to a number of dreadful confrontations. The 51 (H) Division "left hook" burnt out at St Honorine. In the centre, Canadian tanks were badly mauled at Le Mesnil-Patry on 11 June, as were elements of the 3rd Canadian Infantry Division and 46 Royal Marine Commandos at Rots. The initiative petered out on both sides in mutual exhaustion. The "right hook" of the 7th Armoured Division (the "Desert Rats") got as far as Villers Bocage, but the superior armour of the Germans drove them back. (This was their first defeat since El Alamein.) So, the double encirclement of Caen was halted and the main thrust of the battle was switched further west towards the American sector, to Caumont, where the battle raged until 18 June.

On 15 June the V1 attacks on London began in earnest. Hitler's hope was that the Allies would be forced to make a decision – either to come to terms or to launch an attack on the Pas de Calais, (he still wrongly believed that this would be the main attack), which would lead to the destruction of the Allied forces. By 17 June Rommel and Rundstedt were hinting to Hitler, at a conference he attended in Normandy, that he should negotiate for an end to the war. Hitler flew back to Berchtesgaden, full of distrust.

Montgomery called for another attack on Caen for 22 June, but this was delayed until the 25th by the storm which damaged the Mulberry and delayed the off-loading of reinforcements and supplies.

Wednesday 7 June

At last dawn broke and we looked around. Things looked rather a shambles for we had taken quite a pasting. Courseulles seemed to be on fire but our little party had suffered no casualties. I heard that we lost only one vehicle. I felt pleased that I wasn't on one of the ships in the bay. They must have had a pretty rough night of it. Now the armour began to pour ashore, tanks, armoured cars and vehicles by the thousand. Bagpipes announced the arrival of the famous 51 Highland Division and, as they

16

marched by, Sgt Foubister, a Scot, couldn't help but give them a cheer. He was sure we were safe now.* As we ate our breakfast which we cooked on our tommy cookers a terrific explosion occurred. Fouby and I lay quite still for some moments. We were quite dazed from the sudden shock. When we looked up we saw that a 3 ton wagon had run on a Tellermine about 50 yards away. The wagon was no more except for the two back wheels and I do believe we also would have been no more had we not been sitting on the edge of our slit trench. Jerry kept reminding us that he still held the wood so we gave him another dose of the RAF. I think he must have some exceedingly strong fortifications in there, probably of the Tobruk shelter type, in which case he will have to be brought out 'by hand'.

Determined efforts had already been made to reduce this strongpoint. The North Shore Regiment of the Canadian 8th Infantry Brigade had tried on the morning of 7 June to clear the woods at Tailleville, but found that the enemy was able to appear or disappear at will, and that the whole area was an underground labyrinth. Higher command decided to release the North Shore Regiment and turned the task of mopping up the stronghold to the 51st (Highland) Division. The 5th Battalion The Black Watch and three AVREs were "sent to attack with the petard, pillboxes at the Radar Station near Douvres-la-Deliverande and to prove the existence of an organized resistance. Boundary wire on the minefield was run over by mistake and two AVREs broke tracks on mines. Both AVREs were set on fire by 50mm fire, one exploded. The remaining AVRE returned having survived six hits. Majority of crews escaped from tanks and regained own lines." (War Diary 5th Assault Regiment R.E. WO 171/1800, 7 June, 1944) The radar station was going to be a tough nut to crack.

For the rest of the day we sat and watched troops going up to the front. By now the Cdns had two brigades ashore, 3 Br Div also two and the 51st, one. 1 Corps had done very well indeed and if Jerry didn't make his effort soon he would never eject us. Prisoners began to stream back to the beaches. They don't look much like the super race to me, although I believe the 716 Inf Div

---

* When my father's unit pushed on into Germany, Sgt Foubister, quite by chance, came aross his own brother's freshly dug grave. He did not even know that his brother had been killed. The grave of Pte John Foubister (Argyll & Sutherland Highlanders) is in the Rheinberg War Cemetery.

are a pretty poor quality div anyway. The night was just a repeat of the previous one. Jerry put quite an amount of aircraft up and did quite an amount of damage. A few of our ships were hit, supplies and vehicles were set on fire. The Navy was having a tough job for the sea was still very rough. They cannot offload as quickly as they would like. It appears that the 5 Assault Regt RE in their AVREs reached Caen on D Day but were unable to stay as they couldn't get the necessary infantry support they required. The weather was dead against us.

This may be true, but there is no mention of it in the War Diary. In Caen: Anvil of Victory Alexander McKee writes: "Of all the land forces engaged on June 6th, one unit only had reached its set objective, and not merely reached it, but gone beyond it. This was ... the 6th Canadian Armoured Regiment, spearheading 3rd Canadian Infantry Division as flank cover to the assault on Caen ... C Squadron had got on to the final objective, the Caen-Bayeux highway, and pushed on through Bretteville l'Orgueilleuse without orders almost to Carpiquet, the air-field of Caen, ten miles inland. But the infantry had been unable to keep up, and the tanks had been forced to withdraw for the night ... Soon, Kurt Meyer's grenadiers were to be in Carpiquet, and it was to take the Canadians more than four weeks to drive them out. Static warfare was to set in, but no one knew it then." (Pan Books Ltd, London, 1972, pp. 74–75) This thrust may lend a little credence to the exaggerated British newspaper claims of street fighting in Caen on 6 June.

Thursday 8 June
Sleep was again impossible last night and I am beginning to feel a little tired. Chief Engineer's Branch HQ 1 Brit Corps were now complete and we managed to open up shop. Information began to filter through. Corps Tps RE had done a fine job at mine clear-ance, road repairs and hasty bridging. 105 Corps Fd Pk Coy RE were actually established as far forward as La Deliverande so perhaps shortly we will be pushing on. 6 Airborne Div had secured the bridge at Ranville and their operation was a complete success. Men and material are still pouring ashore; soon the bridgehead will blow up like a balloon and burst all over Jerry. He is still holding out in the wood and is proving to be quite a thorn in our side.* I slept in the afternoon in my trench and on

* The 240 Field Company, R.E., engaged at Tailleville on minesweeping the road verges, laying of tank tracks and digging graves with a bulldozer,

being awakened I was informed we had been bombed and shelled. I wouldn't like to miss anything. We were bombed and shelled again this night. It was terribly cold too, so we had rum to drink.

Friday 9 June
Our food is a lot better now for we are feeding from Compo packs. The biscuits are not so good though. I wish we could get another blanket. One is insufficient during these cold nights. In the afternoon the HQ moved to La Deliverande. German aircraft interfered, but missed and as we approached this small Normandy town we were sniped. An M.P. was killed; the sniper was dealt with by a party of Commandos. La Deliverande was a pretty little place, before June 6th. It was a little battle-scarred just now, although the beautiful 'basilique' had very little damage. The people welcomed us and we gave them bully and biscuits and cigarettes. Clear weather enabled the RAF to keep up the good work.

Saturday 10 June
We now seem to be holding a firm bridgehead with our troops disposed as follows: 3 Cdn Div on a line Courseulles – Banville – Reviers – Bény-sur-Mer – Basly – La Deliverande – Langrune. 3 Br Div on a line Cresserons – Plumetot – Hermanville. 51 (H) Div are concentrated in the Orne valley and in contact with 6 Airborne Div in the Ranville, Herouvillette, Escoville area. 30 Corps are on our right and to the right of them the Americans. The Americans also did very well and appear to be advancing on Bayeux with only light opposition. Caen is holding up our advance for Jerry has managed to concentrate some of his Panzer divs in that area. His 716 Inf Div which were our opponents on D Day seems to have been wiped out completely and we are now up against another poor quality div – the 16 GAF (*German Air Force*), which is made up of air force personnel.

Sunday 11 June
A nasty change in the weather grounds our RAF just at the time

---

complain in their War Diary on June 8th of "occasional sniping from nearby wood." (War Office: War Diary 240 Field Company Royal Engineers: WO171/1600, 8 June, 1944.)

we need them most, but this doesn't stop his nightly visits. He was at it again last night and Rear HQ 1 Corps got a couple of close ones. La Deliverande was straffed early this morning. I feel very fit but rather tired. I wonder when I shall be able to take my clothes off and have a good night's sleep. Shall we be in trenches for the duration, or shall we be in houses when we capture a decent-sized town? For security reasons I think that Corps HQ will always keep to the woods and fields. We work quite efficiently under canvas and in the Vic wireless lorry, but I don't know how we shall perform in the winter. So far we have had no mail, but the BBC said that the APO greeted us on the beaches with our mail. As a matter of fact the old BBC news has not altogether hit the mark every time and our DA & QMG is mighty peeved about it.

Monday 12 June
The wood that was holding us up on D + 1 has turned out to be an exceptionally strong fortification known as a Radar Station and is used as an underground HQ for the GAF. It is very well manned with 88mm guns, strong reinforced concrete pillboxes and must contain some 200 men. It is located at Tailleville and though it is completely surrounded it can keep itself for quite some time. Sniping from the Radar Station is interrupting traffic along the Reviers – Deliverande road and so this afternoon the Commandos are out to liquidate it. Lt Col McDowall joins our staff as Airfield Construction adviser. He seems to be quite a perfect gentleman. We seem to have concentrated a terrific AA barrage in the bridgehead these days and at night time it is like a Brock firework display.

Tuesday 13 June
The Commando attack on the Radar Station was unsuccessful and so the RA are having a turn today.

The 41 Royal Marine Commando War Diary records: "On the morning of the 12th . . . it was decided that a fighting patrol commanded by Lieut. Stevens from A Tp. should make an attempt to enter the small station and depending upon success occupy it. For this purpose support was provided by Corps in the shape of the 5th Ass. Sqn. R.E. . . . It was directed by the Corps Commander Lieut. General J.T. Crocker that should the station be occupied by the enemy, the patrol was to withdraw and not suffer unnecessary casualties.

"13 June. 0100 hrs C.S.M. O'Neill and party commence to blow gap; this was successfully completed and at 0200 hrs the (6) AVREs had moved up and were firing off their Petards. On completion A Tp. entered the outer wire and Lieut. Stevens with two men went forward to blow the inner wire. On the explosion of the Bangalore the enemy who up to this time had not fired a single shot opened up with M.G. and Machine Carbine fire from four directions. A fire fight then went on for about a quarter of an hour, the enemy firing very wildly. At about 0300 Lieut. Stevens withdrew his patrol as had been laid down. No casualties were suffered. The enemy retaliated on completion with mortar and shell fire." (ADM 202/103, 12–13 June, 1944)

Brig Campbell our Chief Engineer* thinks it will have to be a job for our Assault Engineers, but we will see if the Field Regt RA can blast them out. A batch of German prisoners came in today. The people of La Deliverande gave them a nasty reception and the MPs had to control the angry crowd. I'm getting a little more sleep now and today I even washed a shirt. 1 Corps are now concentrating and building up. The sea is still too rough for good disembarkation although the Navy claims 23,000 tons unloaded yesterday.† The *Rodney* and *Warspite* have begun to pump shells into Caen and their incessant bombardment all day long gets rather irritating at times.

Wednesday 14 June
Field Regt RA failed to make much impression on Radar Station and so they are continuing to harass our transport. Looks as though 5 Aslt RE will have to take them on after all. American planes bomb Carpiquet airfield, near Caen and on their return a Marauder was shot down. All the occupants parachuted to safety but the plane, without a pilot, just went round and round for about ½ hour, every circle bringing it nearer to earth. We thought it would crash on us at one time, but no, it fell nearer the beaches. I received some of Mary's letters but they were written before the invasion commenced. I hope she is getting mine OK.

---

* Major-General A.D. Campbell C.B.E., D.S.O., M.C.
† The build up was already 48 hours behind schedule at this stage, largely due to the weather.

Thursday 15 June
I noticed today that German prisoners were perfumed and had a nasty sickly sweet smell about them. I visited La Deliverande and made the acquaintance of a very nice family, the Soussenbocs. Nine of them sat down to eat the meat ration of a 24–hour pack. I told the boys and they loaded me down with bully and biscuits for them. They were delighted and made quite a feast from it. I saw also in the town 'collaboratrices'; they all had their heads shaven and the townsfolk jeered them as they were marched by.

Friday 16 June
Last night was terrifying. Jerry had an unusually large force of aircraft over the bridgehead. We had many bombs close by. I was on duty in the wireless truck and unable to take cover. The attack lasted almost two hours. Feel pretty rough this morning. Rear HQ 1 Corps had 5 casualties and lost 2 vehicles. It appears to me that if you can't get a nap during the day you get no sleep at all. There is more going on in this war at night than during the day and so the side which keeps awake the longest are bound to win.

Saturday 17 June
Pleased to announce today that the 5 Assault Regt RE sent in 1 Sqn and captured the Radar Station. The job was beautifully executed and the German Commander still cannot believe that the sappers got through the minefields. He ought to ask his intelligence people for some dope on our secret weapons. They are a little behind the times. These sappers in AVREs [special tanks] and Flails smashed their way through the outer defences and got right on top of the underground stronghold, then with hand-placed charges they blew hell out of it. Their casualties were fairly light I believe, one AVRE and crew being blown up on a mine. The CE (*Chief Engineer*) is delighted, but nothing can be published in the newspapers because they are still on the secret list. There were 200 prisoners taken, plus their lady friends. The place was very lavish inside, containing underground hospital, cinema, and the very delicate machinery they had for detecting both our aircraft and our ships at sea. There was enough food to withstand a siege for a year and I think that we are all going to get a spring mattress for our trenches.

The Radar Station was held by 238 men of Luftnachrichten Regiment

53 and was defended by sixty anti-tank guns, seven flak guns, one mortar and about twenty machine guns, barbed wire and a minefield. It had been built by the Todt Organisation (press-ganged foreign labour) between the end of 1942 and 1943, and was comprised of five radars and about thirty concrete works. It covered twenty acres.

The plan was basically that outlined by my father, but with a period of ten minutes of petarding the concrete defences before the engineers, shrouded in a smoke screen, placed their beehive explosives on the underground targets. The infantry assault was then provided by 41 R.M. Commando. Most textbooks credit the commandos with this victory. The expedition was under the command of Lt. Col. Palmer, 41 R.M. Commando, but the facts from the War Diaries speak for themselves.

This "Account of Operations against Radar Strongpoint at Douvres-la-Deliverande, 17 June, 1944," comes from the 5th Assault Regiment R.E. War Diary: "The action was entirely successful and went very much according to plan but took much longer than was anticipated. Selected approaches were good and generally CRABS were successful, but the four or five casualties they sustained were on mines. Two casualties occurred to AVREs from mines on flailed lanes. The Petard was highly successful but about 30% of rounds failed to explode . . . One Petard scored a direct hit on 50mm in an open emplacement at 60 yards range. 70 lbs Beehives – only about six usefully employed. These were most effective although one failed to penetrate the 10 ft thick roof of one shelter . . . Casualties to AVREs – one blown up, three cas due to 50mm fire." (Op. cit. 17 June, 1944)

According to the 41 R.M. Commando diarist, the assault troops went in after the flail and AVRE operations at 1740 hours. "By this time the enemy had been dazed, shocked or frightened into surrender and came out in large numbers with their hands up. The assault was similarly successful on the small station which was found to contain 38 Germans. The bag in all was 5 officers and 222 O.R.s. A Tp. suffered the only casualty, one man wounded. In all, 44 tanks had taken part in the assault, all was over by 1830 hrs." (Op. cit. 17 June, 1944)

During our 1985 pilgrimage to Normandy, with the help of a large scale map and local people, we were able to locate the remains of the radar station in the middle of cornfields. Today, part of the station has been turned into a museum, but at that time there had been no such restoration. It was a perfect day – a shimmering heat. It felt strange to wander over the now innocent looking lumps of overgrown concrete and rusty steel. It was bizarre to watch our then six-year-old son clambering over the ruins, teddy bear in hand, and to reflect on how much

23

anxiety this place had caused to the grandfather he had never known.

Sunday 18 June
Letter from Mary. She reports on the invasion and knows I am in it, but so far has had no news from me – blast the APO. She is, of course, worried stiff, poor darling. Other chaps have received letters just the same. The DA&QMG is going to make an extensive inquiry into the reason for our mail not reaching home. Bad weather once again. Last night it rained and the water seeped into my trench. Everything got saturated and I finished the night in the cab of the wireless truck.

Monday 19 June
Our troops are now nicely concentrated for a new push. The build-up has been slowed down by the bad weather. There looks like being a big tank battle for Jerry now has opposite us his 21st Panzer Div, 2 Panzer Lehr*, Waffen SS, 816 Panzer Grenadier Div, 15 and 16 GAF Divs and elements of Hitler Jugend. 30 Corps have done about the same as we and now 8 Corps and 12 Corps have almost completed landing. They will come through us at the crucial moment and are at present forming up in our rear. Jerry has all the good positions but I think that our weight of equipment will be too strong for him.

Tuesday 20 June
Jerry bombed our troops concentrations last night. Two huge petrol dumps went up. In the afternoon I went with the Brigadier to see two bridges built by Corps Tps RE over the Caen canal. We crossed over the bridges but not too far. En route I saw where 6 Airborne Div had landed. It was a terrific sight. Hundreds of gliders littered the countryside, some were smashed to blazes and others had made a perfect landing. I think those chaps should have had a VC each.[†] I wonder if Rex was amongst them.

---

* Panzer Lehr was probably the most formidably equipped armoured formation in Normandy at that time, with fast Mark IVs backed up by a heavy tank battalion of Tigers and Panthers and other specialized armour. It was commanded by Rommel's former chief-of-staff in Africa, General-Leutnant Fritz Bayerlein.

[†] There were no VCs, but between 6 June and 14 July the 6th Airborne Division won ten DSOs, twenty MCs, three DCMs, and twenty-two MMs.

Wednesday 21 June

Better flying weather today, even Jerry came over in the daylight. I saw one FW 190 accidentally run into 12 Spitfires. He came down without much ado. Poor Rear HQ got bombed again last night. They are so far behind us that we ask them if they are still sending their washing home. They've had more bombing than we have. La Deliverande was shelled this morning and there were a few casualties. The roads in the bridgehead are causing a lot of trouble. They just can't be expected to stand up to all this traffic, so the CE has written an instruction on road maintenance and in some cases construction – if only the army were all sappers.

At its peak, a main road in this sector at this time would be carrying 13,000 vehicles a day in one direction with 5,200 coming back. Attempts were made to make tanks use diversions to keep them off the hard surfaced roads, but according to the War Diary of the Commander Royal Engineers, 3rd Canadian Infantry Division: "Chief Engineer 1st Corps phoned to say he was not satisfied with road maintenance being done on 'A' route . . . None of the Fd Coys are doing particularly good work on the maintenance of routes. This is probably due to a natural dislike of a routine job by personnel who have been highly trained in an assault role, and to the discouraging fact that neither the Provost nor the Armd Corps units passing through the Divisional area fully realise that tanks should not use surfaced roads but should use tank diversions. This should be taken up very strongly as the condition of the roads is rapidly deteriorating." (Op. cit. 25 June, 1944) Another problem arose from the fact that Caen, with its excellent quarries, had not yet been captured. It had been hoped that this hard stone would have been available. As it was, only a soft limestone was available, which was useless for this particular job.

Thursday 22 June

Gordon Highlanders of the 51 (H) Div attacked a village called St Honorine which the Germans have heavily fortified. This village is of strategic importance and en route to Caen and Colombelles. The attack so far has been tough going but the Scots have got in and are hanging on. We will have to see how the German counter-attack goes on. They are up against 14 GAF. I'll back the Gordons.

St Honorine had already been attacked by the Camerons on 13 June, but they had been badly bruised by a German counter-attack, and they

25

*had been sitting in a defensive position outside the village ever since.
The attack mentioned here actually took place on 23 June and was
largely carried out by the Camerons. But, according to the War Diary
of the 5th Battalion Queen's Own Cameron Highlanders, it was, as my
father suggests, a desperate fight with great losses. At the end of
the day, the village was held and the Camerons were relieved by the
Seaforth Highlanders.*

The Hun has now got properly organised and resistance is stiff-
ening all along the front. Our two divs are having to fight for
every foot of ground. Two nasty spots, Cazelle and Château de la
Londe on the Douvres – Caen roads are definitely a stopping
block. Both these places have withstood two onslaughts already.
It appears that hull down Tiger tanks are taking all we can give
them.*

Friday 23 June
Had quite a good talk to my friends in the village. Although they
don't like the Germans, they admit that they never suffered any
harm from them and that their manner and bearing were always
correct. There has been a severe shortage of food as the bulk of it
was claimed by the German army. In this district also there were
elements of the Todt organisation and recently Normandy was
honoured by a visit of Field Marshal Rommel. He came to see the
defence works. He left a very unfavourable report and this
resulted in every able-bodied man or woman being put to work
on the coast defences. Refusal meant deportation to Germany and
work in munition factories. Most people in the village seem to
have some relative working in Germany. Also, they are all afraid
that the Germans may return and punish them for being friendly
to the English. There are still many pro-German people in this
little town. Only yesterday, the Mayor was arrested by the
Maquis.

Saturday 24 June
51 (H) Div got kicked out of St Honorine with fairly heavy casualties too, but they'll have another try soon. 3 Br Inf Div got
nettled also at Lebisey Wood. There is a small factory in this wood
and Jerry thinks quite a deal of it. Maybe it will be another Radar

* Tiger tanks driven into a man-made pit so that only the turret was
visible. The tank still usually had a 360° circle of fire.

26

Station job. This afternoon Corps HQ moved to Douvres-la-Deliverande on the Caen road. The Brigadier's caravan is nicely fitted into a huge 'slit trench' made by a bulldozer; we had to bury a horse before we could settle down. There are lots of stray horses about this district. The Germans were forced to use this animal owing to transport difficulties. Our Lt Col Poole, DSO, MC has a beautiful charger which once belonged to some German officer. We are still being subjected to nightly bombing attacks and our AA defences are simply terrific. I much prefer to be down here than up there. I wonder how any plane can fly through such flak. Occasional short sharp air battles send us scurrying out into the open to get an eyeful. We should hate to miss anything, but the Brig takes a poor view of us exposing ourselves and plays merry hell if he sees us.

Chapter Three

Epsom, Windsor and Charnwood – the Battle for Caen

Once more troops had been landed, a larger scale attack was possible. Epsom was designed to sweep three Corps (30, 8 and 1 Corps from west to east), around the west of Caen in a massive right hook. Because some units had a greater distance to cover, there was to be a staggered start, with the outer (western) rim of the wheel starting out first on 25 June. They would cross the rivers Odon and Orne, push on and capture the heights to the south of the city, and thereby squeeze the Germans out of Caen. In the process the Canadians were to seize Carpiquet airfield and the 51st Highland Division was to break out of the Airborne bridgehead and attack the city from the east. The road would then be open to Falaise. In the main, new, fresh troops were involved in the fighting.

The Allies were faced (from the German left to right) by elements of Panzer Lehr, 12th SS and 26th Panzer Regiments and the 25th SS Panzer Grenadier Regiment. The weak point was the centre. The 12th SS had been decimated and was largely made up of teenagers (Hitler Jugend), who were facing the weight of 60,000 men, 600 tanks and 700 guns of 8 Corps.

The nature of the bocage countryside, with its limited vision, meant that the sweep turned into a ragtag of hundreds of skirmishes between individual groups. Warfare in this kind of terrain suited the defenders rather than the attackers. The West Riding Division on the outside of the wheel did not reach all its first-day objectives, so the centre of the attack (the 15th Scottish Division) was raked by enemy fire from high ground when they attacked the next day, 26 June.

28

Attack after attack was held by German Panthers, but on 27 June the Argyll & Sutherland Highlanders of the 15th Scottish Division broke through to a bridge over the Odon and on to Hill 112. This wedge, 6 miles deep and 2 miles wide, became known as the Battle of the Scottish Corridor.

There were stiff counter-attacks in the corridor on the 29th and the battle went back and forth with great ferocity. The sweep had halted. The Germans had held the initial advance with whatever resources they could lay their hands on, followed up by reinforcements which were arriving from the Eastern Front. Meanwhile, the Allies were experiencing great difficulty in getting armour up to the front on roads which were choked with traffic and breaking down under the weight of armour.

Epsom had failed, but the overall plan was working in that the British and Canadians were attracting the attentions of seven and a half Panzer Divisions, while the Americans at this time were faced by only half a division. The British and Canadians contented themselves with just holding the line, to let the main German counter-attack from 29 June onwards exhaust itself, using up precious reserves, and buying the Americans valuable time. While all this was going on, the warships off the Normandy coast were lobbing heavy shells on to the German counter-attack with devastating effect. It was said that one of these shells landing near a 56–ton Panther could flip the tank onto its side just from the blast.

Operation Windsor was the plan for the Canadian 8th Infantry Brigade to capture Carpiquet village and airfield. Although these were held by very small numbers, the attack was countered and held in the first few days by elements of the 25th Panzer Grenadier Regiment, who had the advantage of strong, underground blockhouses, connected by passages. German radio intelligence was listening in to Canadian wireless messages, and having access to the codes, were forewarned of each move. Defensive fire from German artillery and mortars inflicted very heavy casualties among the Canadians.

On 4 July, the main attack went in and the village was captured, but the Canadians were held in situ for the next few days, and were still fighting defensively when the main attack on Caen began on 7 July.

Epsom and Windsor therefore, had both ground to a halt, but the next plan was less subtle – a head-on attack on the city with huge air and artillery support, codenamed Charnwood.

To secure the capture of Caen, there was to be an assault by 3 divisions on 8 July – the inexperienced 59th Division from the north, with 3rd British Infantry Division on the left flank, supported by the 3rd

Canadian Infantry Division and the 51st Highland Division on the right. The assault was to be supported by a terrific artillery barrage, with the battleships piling in their weight for good measure. But this was preceded on 7 July by a huge aerial bombardment, designed to sweep away the enemy defences. However, the main German defences were too close to the Allied front line for safety (a gap of at least 6,000 yards was needed), so the most that the bombardment could do was to disrupt German communications to their main defensive line in northern Caen. The defensive line itself remained relatively intact. The raid is largely considered to have been futile, the ancient city of Caen paying the price in its buildings and citizens. The damage in fact hindered the Allied advance once they got into the city.

The main attack went in on 8 July and on the 9th, the 3rd British Division finally moved into the city from the east and the 3rd Canadian from the west. The German defenders retired across the River Orne to Colombelles and the Faubourg de Vaucelles. Caen was largely liberated, but the vital high ground to the south of the city, across the river, was still in German hands.

Sunday 25 June

At last I hear that Mary has received my letters. This news came as a great relief, for I am sure that my letters put her mind at rest; they were meant to anyway. A letter from mother tells me that she is a little sceptical about the easy time I told her. She sends her blessing and prays for me. Mother always could read through me. Rex *did* come over with the Airborne Div. I must try and visit him somehow. Our line is slowly closing in on Caen, but Jerry is packing in some SS Divs and more armour. I'm sure that our two divs must be feeling the strain of continuous fighting since D Day. German planes have been seen taking off from Carpiquet airfield, near Caen. It has always been assumed that this was knocked out long ago.

Monday 26 June

After last night I have decided to make a good job of my slit trench. I must get a good cover on it for the shrapnel simply rains down. It also wants revetting as the vibration from the guns causes the sides to come in. Nice little push by the Cdns has put them astride the Caen–Bayeux road and the capture of Rots. 3 Br also were having a go last night but Lebisey Wood still held fast. Another thorn down that way is a small village called Galmanche. Tigers dig in once more.

Tuesday 27 June
What a night. The rain came down in torrents and flooded our slit trenches. Then it stopped about three o'clock and we sat about until Jerry came. He dropped some very close ones and we were glad to get in the trench, water or no water. I've managed to scrounge a piece of Armco Culverting for head cover. This will hold 40 tons so I think I will sleep well tonight. The Intelligence Officer of 6 Airborne Div was killed on a mine yesterday. He was a grand fellow too. It seems hard luck after going through that landing to meet such an ignoble end.

*I think that this must be Captain F.C. Scholes, though he was killed a little earlier than my father suggests. He was held in high esteem by others too, including the Commanding Officer of 6th Airborne Division who wrote: "He showed a wonderful sense of his responsibilities; his detail was excellent; his statements always accurate; and his deductions in consequence were sound. But poor Freddie was killed whilst at work. I personally felt his loss most keenly. He was a great Christian and a good man. By profession a schoolmaster, the youth of our country has indeed lost something that in these overcast days of doubt and uncertainty would have been invaluable. Perhaps his spirit is at work somewhere doing good and helping others still." (*With the 6th Airborne Division in Normandy *by Lt. Gen. R.N. Gale, Sampson Low, Marton & Co. Ltd., London, 1948, p. 113) He is buried in Ranville Military Cemetery, Normandy.*

Wednesday 28 June
I had to abandon my trench again last night for once more the tide came in. I slept under the office wagon and slept very well too for, for the first time since D Day I took my clothes off to sleep. Jerry came again as usual but I ignored him and so he went away. Douvres was today given a beating up by shells and there was quite an amount of damage and a few casualties. None of the shells fell in the Corps HQ area, but I suppose he has been DF-ing us.* These wirelesses are a menace at times. Our 4th Commando is having fun at Sallenelles with the

* Direction finding. Two radio stations tuned to the frequency of the enemy station and separated by some miles from one another. By using a directional aerial, the signal of maximum volume is received when the aerial is pointing directly at the offending station. When plotting this line for each of the two separate stations on a map, the point at which the two lines cross is the location of the enemy station.

31

Wehrmacht. Commandos occupy it by night and retire before dawn when Jerry is allowed to return. These Commandos make Jerry very jittery and during patrols the Heinies fire at each other.

Thursday 29 June

Without a word of warning the Gordons got mad with St Honorine and assisted by the RA set about the place and took it for a good an' all last night, although the place is reduced to a shambles; their casualties were pretty heavy though. So was Jerry's – he also lost 300 prisoners. Anyway, that is one nasty spot cleared up. Cdns captured Le Bourg and should soon be able to have a crack at Carpiquet. The Germans have thrown a ring of steel around the north of Caen. Our two battleships haven't stopped shelling the place since about D + 2. We take it as a matter of course these days.

Friday 30 June

We must admit, old Jerry is holding us in a grip of iron. If we can only break through at one point and deploy our troops a rout will set in. As it is we have no room to turn round. The bridgehead is absolutely packed out with troops. We are smothering ourselves. When Jerry bombs he can't help but hit something. Lebisey Wood, Château de la Londe, La Bijude, Colombelles, Authie, and Carpiquet are holding all our attempts to break them. 3 Br Inf Div are having heavy casualties too. The Norfolks are bashing themselves up against La Bijude every day without making much headway. Typhoons are doing marvellous work against these defences but these Germans are tough. Monty is in the thick of it every day. He is a most remarkable General and I think he'll fox the enemy yet.

Saturday 1 July

Had a trip out with Brig Campbell. What an eye-opener this bridgehead is. The roads are no more than rubble, every village is a torn wreck, thousands of troops are bivouacing in the fields awaiting the big push on Caen. Tanks, guns, lorries, dumps, hospitals, mechanical eqpt, DUKWs (*amphibious trucks*) and jeeps by the thousand milling about the place. Only a Brigadier with his priority vehicle and loud voice can get around this place. We visited the bridges at Ranville and continued into the 6 Airborne Div territory. I managed to find Rex, nicely dug in and to attract his attention I had to shout. This, to a Lt didn't look too good in front of the Brig, but I wanted to see Rex. We had quite a good talk together and exchanged some good yarns. These Airborne troops are tough. They've had a heluva time and actually I think that they should be withdrawn to England, but according to the Brig they will be soon acting in the role of a light inf div.

Sunday 2 July
The Luftwaffe fancied its chances today and we saw quite a number of skirmishes. Jerry is trying to find out our troop dispositions for he knows that there is something afoot. Our Divs are nicely built up now and we are planning the next move which is the ultimate capture of Caen. The Cdns have to try and get right behind it from the Bayeux side, 3 Br will go straight in with 5 Assault Regt RE as spearhead, 51 (H) Div will continue down towards Giberville. If we don't get out of this bridgehead soon we will be suffering from claustrophobia.

Monday 3 July
Another rough night. The whole area seems to have been heavily bombed. I thought it would never stop as I sat in the Vic. One bomb anywhere near that truck and we've had it. It rocked about like a cockle boat as the concussion struck it. The Cdns have at last made a move, brilliantly executed too. Early this morning they attacked Carpiquet and the airfield.* First reports told of heavy casualties on both sides. Our friends the Chaudières along with the Queen's Own Rifles of Canada were the first in. Their opponents are two SS Panzer Grenadier Divs, the 11 and 9th. These two German Divs operated in North Africa – quite seasoned troops. I noticed from the G information room that our famous 7th Armoured Division has been switched to the Tilly-sur-Seulles district in order to meet their old enemies 21 SS Panzer Div whom they chased from El Alamein to Tunis. I believe just now that this is the scene of the bloodiest fighting.

Tuesday 4 July
Our 3 Cdn Inf Div managed to capture the village of Carpiquet and half the airfield, but their losses have been exceedingly heavy and just now it is touch and go whether or not they can hold it as

* The opening of Operation Windsor and it should read 4 July.

33

Jerry is rushing up more and more reserves, including those fanatics of the Hitler Jugend. Until this village is taken for good our other Divs won't make a move.

The plan for the attack on Carpiquet by the 8th Canadian Infantry Brigade was in two phases. The capture of the village and northern side of the airfield by the North Shore Regiment and Régiment de la Chaudière, was to be followed by the Queen's Own Rifles of Canada passing through the village and capturing the control buildings on the east. The Royal Winnipeg Rifles of 7th Brigade were to seize the southern hangars.

The Chaudières advanced on the village under the cover of an enormous barrage provided by the artillery and 16 inch shells from HMS Rodney and HMS Roberts. The enemy was well organized in camouflaged trenches and gun emplacements with 6 feet thick reinforced walls and roofs. Crocodiles were needed to clear these nigh impregnable positions. The village was captured with heavy casualties and Battalion H.Q. were set up in a German dug-out. Panthers counter-attacked, but were repulsed. But the Winnipegs had to withdraw from their objective for the enemy was too strongly dug in, and the second phase was not carried out. At the end of 4 July the control buildings and the southern hangars were still in enemy hands with over 320 casualties for the 8 Brigade. The battle is famous in Canadian military history. In Le Geste du Régiment de la Chaudière *it is written: "On our side as on the German, we took no prisoners that day." (By Majors A. Ross and M. Gauvin, Holland, 1945, p. 39)*

Everything is at high tension just now and soon the storm will break. Either Jerry will have a go at pushing us back into the sea (which he still maintains he can do) or else we'll take Caen. Caen has a population of 65,000 and it is believed that the Germans will not allow the civilians to evacuate. They know too much about the defences.

This must have been a rumour. According to A. McKee, as early as 8 June M. Cacaud (Prefect) and A. Detoile (Mayor) had signed an evacuation notice saying: "Owing to the murderous bombardments which are making our city a city of death, we strongly advise those who have no official or administrative charge to evacuate." And on 17 June a nun of the Bon Sauveur Convent wrote in her diary: "Today it is rumoured that everyone must leave Caen." (A. McKee Op. cit. p. 133) On 29 June evacuation of the city was urged again. The Germans pulled out

*many of their own officials and the Gestapo, so that only fighting
soldiers were left, and convicts were allowed out of the prisons. On a
recent visit to Normandy, M. Jean Guillot of Nonant, near Bayeux,
told me that in the weeks before and after the liberation of Caen, the
population of Nonant (about 200) was swelled by a further 300
Caennais. At this time it was essential to milk the cows to feed the extra
children, even during the height of the fighting and all the dangers that
that entailed.*

Close to Caen is a very large factory that is almost a small town
in itself, Colombelles. We've given that place some hammer from
the air and from the Gunners. The Germans have made it into a
formidable strongpoint.

Wednesday 5 July
Heavy German counter-attack as was expected at Carpiquet
retakes the airfield and practically wipes out the Cdn 8th Bde, but
Jerry didn't get it all his own way either for the Cdns badly mauled
his Jugend. They won't hold it long for the weather, according to
our Met section, is on the mend and we will be able to put the
Lancasters on them.

*Losses were heavy, but the 8th Brigade managed to hold on by the skin
of their teeth during the ensuing days. "For five days Carpiquet was a
hell. Mortars, rockets and artillery fired non stop. There was not an
inch of ground which was not touched. The bombardment was so
continuous that a man scarcely dare leave his trench." (Ross and
Gauvin Op. cit. p. 40) On 5 July the Chaudières H.Q. received three
direct hits. An attempt to lay a defensive minefield under such heavy
fire was impossible. On the 6th, with mounting losses, C Company had
to evacuate. But in spite of lack of sleep and the constant bombardment, positions were held. The final push, codenamed "Trousers" and
scheduled for the 8th, was postponed until the 9th. At 7.40 p.m. on 8
July Tactical H.Q. of 3rd Canadian Division signalled, "Trousers off
until tomorrow". On 9 July after an artillery barrage, the attack was
made on the last enemy held hangars. By midday their objective
was finally captured.*

Jerry celebrated his success by bashing us again with his guns
from Lebisey Wood. We took to our holes and stayed there for
some time. It's queer but I never dream of getting hit. Our
draughtsman couldn't stand the racket and his nerves went all

haywire; he's back in England now, we think. He gave me the willys when he started on one of his nervous rounds.

Thursday 6 July
More shelling of this area and a few civilians and a horse got killed. The Navy have increased their bombardment on Caen and are simply pouring shells across; 4 AGRA have got their 5.5s opposite Château de la Londe and La Bijude; 90 Field Regt RA are all set to take on Lebisey Wood; 3 Br Inf Div and 5 Aslt Regt are nicely positioned. There appears to be a lull before the storm.

Friday 7 July
At 0800 hrs this morning we had a breathtaking sight. 700 Lancasters dropped 5,000 tons of bombs on Caen taking about 1½ hrs to do it. I've never heard such a din. It was worse than D Day. At first they were met by heavy flak and two or perhaps three came down in flames, but after about ½ hour the flak was no more. Completely saturated, huge columns of smoke rose from Caen as this magnificent city was given a death blow. I felt a little sorry for the civilians in there, but this bombing will save us many troops. It had to be done.

This was the opening of Operation Charnwood. The timing given by my father for the bombing raid caused me some difficulties. Most sources suggest an evening attack, but even these disagree. The War Diary for the 7th Canadian Infantry Brigade says: "In the evening a vast droning noise filled the sky – everyone was hugely excited . . . 450 heavy bombers with suitable fighter escort roared overhead and attacked targets in NW Caen. Morale effect on the troops one hundred per cent – everyone trying to get grandstand seats for the show. Flak was heavy at first but slackened off as weight of our bombs was felt. Got to hand it to the boys in blue – they are really doing a job." (WO 179/2879, 7 July, 1944) Le Geste du Régiment de la Chaudière gives the time as 6.00 p.m. while Colonel C.P. Stacey in his The Victory Campaign writes that the attack lasted from 9.50 to 10.30 p.m., though he also points out that Air Chief Marshall Leigh-Mallory's despatch erroneously states that the attack went in at 4.30 a.m. on 8 July. So there is obviously some confusion. Certainly there was heavy bombing at the time my father suggests, for Luce Triboulet in her book Pour Retrouver Mon Fils à Caen, describes hiding in the cellar on the morning on 7 July while the ground shook during the raid. They placed pillows over their faces for they knew of some people who had been blinded by flying debris. On that same occasion a two-ton bomb landed fifteen yards from their cellar killing fifty six people and caving in ten houses.

The likelihood of high civilian casualties caused argument and dissension within higher command. Churchill and the British War Cabinet opposed the blitz but were overruled by Roosevelt who said that, though the loss of civilian lives was regrettable, he could not impose restrictions on military action which might militate against the success of the operation. General Bradley had himself ordered: "If it becomes necessary to save time, put 500 or even 1,000 tons of air on the place and take the city apart." (Quoted in McKee, Op. cit. pp 139–140)

The bombing in fact had a negligible effect on the actual defences to the north of the city, and an Allied investigation by a team that arrived in Caen on 12 July, 1944, said there was little evidence of German artillery batteries or other targets listed by the Second British Army. What in fact the raid did do was to alert the German defenders to the imminent attack.

When the bombing ceased the artillery opened up with the biggest barrage of the war. About a thousand big guns belched forth fire and steel.* This barrage began at 10.00 hrs and is still on as I write this. It is not due to finish until 22.00 hrs tonight. I'm sure my other ear will seize up on me soon. I haven't got the first ear trouble right yet. Well we must see how the boys go on tomorrow when at 0700 hrs they begin phase 1 in the capture of Caen.

Saturday 8 July
At 0700 hrs 1 Corps, with 3 Br Inf Div, 3 Cdn Inf Div and 51 (H) Div attacked Caen. The former coming in from the north with the other two divs on either flank, each div had two brigades up, elements of 5 Aslt Regt RE forming the spearhead of each attack. Lebisey Wood was over-run early on and Galmanche succumbed to the Royal Ulster Rifles. This was great news from 3 Br Inf Div. Then the Cdns said they'd got Carpiquet and the airfield too. The Nazis were stunned by our terrific air and ground bombardment. 51 (H) Div got the remains of Colombelles and were nicely proceeding on to Cuverville and Herouville. That horrible place

* Each gun in the Canadian artillery batteries would fire about 13 tons of shells in this first day of the attack.

Château de la Londe was no more. This was the bitterest fighting of the war I believe. I will never forget the sound of that battle, for into this area, a very small area, was packed the finest men of two of the finest armies in the world. Both sides having much armour, only the RAF could have made it possible for us to take it and even the Navy had to help. Phase 1 was completed when we heard the news that 3 Br Inf Div were fighting in the outskirts of Caen with the magnificent sappers in tanks of the 5 Aslt Regt RE. We must now await further news tomorrow when phase II begins. To round off the day Corps HQ got a shelling from Jerry's long range guns across the Orne.

Sunday 9 July
Phase II went exactly as planned, except for the fact that there was so much debris blocking the roads into Caen that we had to fetch up armoured bulldozers to clear it away. The Royal Ulster Rifles were the first to get to the centre of Caen with the good old Cdns coming in from the other side. Even though the French must have suffered terrific casualties in this city, they gave our troops a remarkable welcome. Their city is absolutely and definitely finished with hardly a building standing except in the south west, where even now a strong German pocket is still holding out.* The Chief Engineer was down in Caen early on and en route he signalled his jeep driver to stop, he entered a house with his revolver at the ready and brought out 5 Nazis. These he loaded into the jeep and brought back to Corps HQ.† Everybody is pleased by our latest advance. We feel as though we have room to stretch a little now. I wonder what the armchair critics are saying at home now about Monty.

Monday 10 July
Caen is out of bounds except to duty personnel, this of course to

* The Chief Engineer's War Diary on 9 July states: "Caen was captured during the course of the afternoon by 3 Br Div. Access was only possible with tracked vehicles owing to bomb damage. Attempts were made to recce the river but failed owing to strength of enemy on far bank until late in evening." (War Diary, Chief Engineer 1st Corps 2nd Army: WO 171/266, 9 July, 1944) The Advance had gone as far as the River Orne, across which all the bridges had been blown.
† The Chief Engineer, Brig. Campbell, must have been too modest to mention this incident in the War Diary. He simply says that he went down the Caen–Bayeux road with Capt. Stewart.

stop sightseers. I doubt if there would be any loot left from all accounts. It is not the ordinary troops who do the looting either.

The Battalion Orders of 11 July to the Royal Regina Rifles were: "Caen is 'Out of Bounds' to everybody except officers and men belonging to 3rd Cdn. Inf. Div. necessarily there on duty. All vehicles except flag cars leaving Caen will be stopped. If necessary they will be searched. Any officer or O.R. caught looting will be tried by FGCM. It is up to the British and Canadian soldiers to preserve discipline and to render assistance in every way to allied people who have already shown their happiness at liberation. LOOTING MUST NOT OCCUR. The people of Caen have had HELL during the past month and deserve every consideration." (War Diary: WO 179/2961, 11 July, 1944)

The same orders were issued to other Canadian units though the Allies were not the culprits according to the War Diary of the 7th Canadian Infantry Brigade. "Caen was our first experience with a city that had really been liberated. The destruction was colossal – and the inhabitants weren't frightfully pleased about it either. We also saw some first class examples of German looting. Houses were in a mess, everything pulled out of the drawers, glass and china smashed, empty bottles everywhere." (op. cit. 10 July, 1944)

Food and medical supplies are getting priority for it is estimated that 3000 civilians were killed and almost double that number wounded. If the army is not careful then a nasty disease can break out after this job. There is no fresh water either, but the RE are erecting 5 water points already.

The population of Caen before the war was about 60,000. On 6 June at 3.00 p.m. there was a violent raid on Caen to destroy German communications which killed and wounded many boys at St Mary's Seminary and school. This prompted many to leave the city and others poured into the convents which were rapidly converted into hospitals. Others lived in the great churches and the cathedral, while several thousand refugees sheltered in the great underground caves of Fleury-sur-Orne. It is not possible to say how many Caennais remained in the city during the battle, or indeed how many were killed. Two thousand tons of bombs were dropped on Caen between 6 June and 18 July. Possibly five thousand civilians were killed, but the actual figure is not known and research still goes on. Where whole families were wiped out, their deaths perhaps went unrecorded.

The unprepared survivors could barely cope. Casualties were especially high among trained firefighters and yet the fires raged for eleven days. The Bon Sauveur nun wrote in her diary after the 7 July raids: "They say that 5,000 are dead. I know that many hundreds are still buried in the debris, still alive. Everyone united in the rescue work, but we were so few, and the number of victims so many, that the task was beyond us. The piteous cries of those we could not reach will haunt us for a long time." (McKee, Op. cit. p 230) Dead civilians were buried in gardens, courtyards or on the roadside, wrapped in sheets or paper. The raids destroyed 75 per cent of the historic city. The old university was one of the first casualties of 7 July. A naval shell from HMS Rodney shattered the steeple of St Pierre. Almost every convent in Caen was hit. But there was one 'safe island'. The Cathedral of St Etienne and the Abbaye-aux-Hommes along with the mental hospital at Bon Sauveur Convent housed hundreds of homeless families, and remained virtually untouched. The Allies struck a deal with the Germans – these central buildings could prevent themselves from becoming targets of RAF raids by painting huge red crosses on the roofs, so long as the Germans did not abuse the arrangement and put their own troops inside too. The bargain was honoured. 2,000 people lived for several weeks in the Abbaye-aux-Hommes. About 20,000 people lived in the centre of the city itself, but in very difficult conditions.

Luce Triboulet's home was near the coast, but on 6 June she was separated from her young son who had gone to Caen for three days to prepare for his first communion. On 22 June she finally got through Allied and German lines and into the city, and found her son sheltering in a convent. Her book (Pour Retrouver Mon Fils à Caen) details their experiences as homeless refugees in the city and their failed attempts to leave. They spent their nights in the Cathedral of St Etienne: "This splendid church was full of refugees, each family had made a kind of small house with a square of chairs, a little straw, some plates, sometimes their bicycles. Everything smelt very strongly of disinfectant. Only the chancel was used for services; a little sermon each evening, often by the Abbé Pelcerf, priest of St Jean . . ." (Caen, 1960, pp 30–31)

Faubourg de Vaucelles in the southern outskirts of Caen below the (*river?*) is still in German hands and he is already getting his artillery to bear on our supply columns. Although we are getting our letters alright, our families at home are not receiving any news from us – I'm about fed up with the APO. They are a disgrace to the RE. As long as Mary gets my letters I don't mind even missing hers. She needs my letters very much just now.*

Tuesday 11 July
We said goodbye to 3 Cdn Inf Div as they are now coming under command of 2 Cdn Corps, which so far is in no army. They are a fine div and have taken on a big chunk of the fighting since D Day. 3 Br Inf Div are moving over to the 6 Airborne Div sector to rest and reform. We are at this location just a few hundred yards from the Radar Station and it is now being used as a training ground for sappers. There are still extensive minefields around the place and this is a fine opportunity to try out new weapons at mine detecting. Today there was a nasty accident in a minefield. Lt Pritchard and Lt Taylor were detecting mines using the Dog Platoon. The dogs set off across the field and quickly found nine mines. The two officers followed when suddenly there was a terrific explosion which blew Mr Taylor 20 ft away. Mr Pritchard had stood on a Schumine and it blew both his legs off. The field was later swept properly and it was found that the dogs had missed 11 mines.† So much has happened recently on 1 Corps front that we have been apt to overlook our American allies. Well, they are doing fine just now. After clearing the Cherbourg peninsula they are pushing south at a good rate and at present are at the gates of St Lô. According to what I remember of the planning in London we have to wait at Caen until they swing right round and face Paris, having cleared the Brest peninsula and captured St Nazaire. This might sound like a lot but our intelligence told us that that country is but weakly held and not until Falaise is in their hands will the British Second Army sweep to the Seine. But of course plans have to be altered a lot to suit the circumstances.

* Apart from being separated by war, my mother was expecting her first baby.
† The date was 12 July and the demonstration was in public. The Chief Engineer's War Diary records: "Demonstration of mine lifting using Dog Platoon to be given 12 July with one sec. 240 Fd Coy Demonstration commences 1000 hrs. at southern half of Radar stronghold. Spectators stand 006804." Later, on the same day: "Report on accident on clearing minefield at Radar Stn.", though no details were given. (Op. cit. 12 July, 1944)

Wednesday 12 July
A sudden heavy counter-attack on Caen from the Vaucelles area was nicely repulsed by the Cdns and we believe it cost Jerry dear. I don't think he can retake Caen now. Water supply is now becoming a serious problem and all our available Fd Coys are engaged on this task.* With 2 Cdn Corps concentrating in the Carpiquet area and 12 Corps to their right, whilst behind them 8 Corps are doing their war dance, I think that the balloon will go up again very soon. Enemy air activity at night still continues and Jerry would sorely love to destroy our bridges over the Caen canal and the River Orne, but we have a good concentration of AA in these places.

Thursday 13 July
General Crerar has now come over and I think that a Cdn Army will be formed. He has sent a personal message to the Cdns not to retaliate on the Germans for their atrocity of murdering 20 Cdn prisoners. It appears that these prisoners were made to dig a trench. They were then lined along the edge of it and cruelly mown down. These defenceless men had dug their own grave. (*See Appendix 1*) I wonder if Gen Crerar heard what the French Cdns did on D + 3 at a little village called Banville. They were advancing through this village when their major was shot dead by a sniper. The sniper was located in a church steeple and winkled out alive. He was then taken into a farmyard, made to kneel and was then beheaded with a woodman's axe.

The church steeple at Banville had already caused problems for 'C' Company of the Royal Winnipeg Rifles. On 6 June they had dealt with six snipers concealed in the tower. Sniping was a constant problem as the War Diary of the 8th Canadian Infantry Brigade records: "Sniping continued and aggressive measures were taken to put a cessation to these activities." (Op. cit. 10 June, 1944) Many churches were purposely demolished because they provided observation posts and harbours for snipers. Roman Catholic tank commanders were selected

* The following orders were issued to the Regina Rifles on 11 July: "(a) As the River Mue is almost the only source of water for troops and civilians in this area, every effort will be made to keep its water free of contamination. (b) No refuse will be dumped nor any latrines or urinals erected in the vicinity of the river. (c) No bathing by personnel, no washing of vehicles and no fording of the river by vehicles will take place for at least one mile above water point." (War Diary, Op cit. 11 July, 1944.)

for the task so that Roman Catholic soldiers could not complain.

But whether my father's story here is true or just a rumour, I cannot tell. Certainly, the French Canadians gained a reputation for ruthlessness. Again, Alexander McKee writing about Bernières on D Day: "Waiting to advance under cover of the sea wall was a French-Canadian regiment which had lost heavily crossing the exposed beach; they were to acquire a reputation, later that day, for having dragged a female collaborator round the village behind a jeep. True, false, or exaggerated, it was a fitting rumour with which to open the ruthless battle of Normandy." (Op. cit. p. 52)

The Russians have made a sudden breakthrough and just now are only 32 miles from East Prussia.

Friday 14 July
I had a couple of hours free this morning so I wandered down to La Deliverande for a look round. Quite a lot has happened to this place since I was last there, for one thing the roads have just about had it. Great masses of armour have literally chewed them up. Then again a lot of the damaged buildings have been rebuilt or repaired. Thousands of troops are simply milling about all over the place – lines of convoys pushing up to the front – Cdns seem to be predominating. They are resting after the recent heavy fighting. The oldest profession too seems to be flourishing again although there are two MPs on guard outside the door. I visited my first friends, Madame Soussenboc's family. They were delighted to see me and the good lady gave me a souvenir by way of a little medallion showing 'Our Lady of Lourdes' which she had had blessed by the priest of the 'basilique', for my good luck.* During the afternoon 3 FW 190s paid us a visit. All three were shot down when they got in the Ranville barrage.

---

* We used La Deliverande as our main base in this part of Normandy during our 1985 trip. Attempts to locate the Soussenboc family unfortunately failed, but I took the little 'Lady of Lourdes' to the basilica, where it was blessed again by the current priest. I always carry it for good luck. After all, it saw my father relatively unscathed through the war.

43

Chapter Four

Goodwood

While the British and Canadians were holding the bulk of the German armour around Caen, the American break-out in the west began on 3 July, but not until 25 July did the break-out occur on the scale hoped for (Operation Cobra).

Between 10 July and 1 August, there was more severe fighting around Hill 112 to the south-west of the city. This so-called "Hill of Calvary" helped to keep German armour occupied. The hill changed hands a number of times and consumed many casualties. Eventually, on 1 August, German Tigers withdrew.

Hitler had, by this time, come to the realization that Normandy and not the Pas de Calais was the main Allied attack. To counter this, he had moved four more divisions into Normandy, three of them facing the British and Canadians. Meanwhile, the Germans began to pull much of the surviving armour out of Caen to mount a massive counter-attack against the Americans. Partly in an attempt to draw that armour back to Caen, emergency measures had to be taken – Operation Goodwood.

The plan was for 8 Corps to break out of the Airborne bridgehead to the east of Caen and mount a swinging 'left hook' around and to the south of the city, seize the high ground (the Bourguebus Ridge) which dominated the Caen Plain, and thus open the way to Falaise. It was to be a swift move by armoured divisions, with British infantry clearing the heavily fortified villages on the left flank, while the Canadians cleared the fortified factory area of Colombelles on the right flank. The bridgehead from which the attack was to be launched was cramped, so it was going to have to be a mad dash by armoured divisions, in file, on a narrow front. The attack was to be preceded by the biggest air raid of the war, followed by an artillery barrage which, it was thought, would pulverize the German defences.

44

The attack went in on 18 July, but, for many reasons, was not as successful as hoped, and the high plateau to the south of the city was only partly taken, with great difficulty, on the 19th. The 11th Armoured Division was exhausted in the process and the impetus behind the armoured drive had gone. The Canadians got bogged down trying to capture the Verrières Ridge on the summit. About 300 tanks were lost in the 3-day period, 18 to 20 July, and some infantry battalions were reduced to half strength.

Cobra began on 25 July, and to make sure that no German divisions were transferred to the American sector, a further onslaught was launched by the Canadians on the Verrières Ridge, at great cost, over several days.

Saturday 15 July

Once more on planning, this time Operation 'Goodwood' which is a push by 8 Corps to the SE of Caen, supported by elements of 1 Corps, especially the engineers who have to construct 3 bridges over the Orne in Caen.* This is to be rather a ticklish job for our RE as the bridges cannot be built until the very last minute, so to speak, for to build them before would give away our intentions to the enemy. They will have to be built the night previous to the morning attack. It is going to be difficult to hide the bridging equipment near to the sites.

As secrecy was all-important, the stores were brought up in advance and hidden near the sites. The bridges were built overnight on 17–18 July. But, in addition, much had to be done to improve the roads. Mine-lifting was difficult and dangerous for many of the mines had been laid early on, in the fluid stage of fighting, by inexperienced troops. There was so much to do that only narrow tracks could be lifted for the armour to use.

Sunday 16 July

Worked all night on planning 'Goodwood'. What a din there too. 8 Corps were moving to their assembly area. Shermans and Churchills streamed past this HQ all night long and of course to add to this Jerry came over and our AA boys put up a terrific show. I had a good long sleep after dinner, then a bath out of a petrol tin. We have a novel way of heating water. First a petrol tin cut in half and filled with earth. On to this is poured petrol and

* Blainville, Ecarde and Longueval.

oil. Allow it to soak a few minutes and hey presto, you have a fire fit to cook a dinner. I bet Jerry would scream with anguish if he saw what we did with this precious fluid.

Monday 17 July

As I was working today I heard the report of a sten gun close by. This is nothing unusual and I took little notice until a few minutes later when one of our Signals operators stumbled into the tent holding his head which was covered in blood. The bullet had entered through his eye and departed by way of his right ear. He was rushed off to the CCS.* We occupy Jerry's mind with plenty of air activity so that 8 Corps can get properly into position for the big attack which is to commence about noon tomorrow. Our sappers are all set for the hasty bridging tonight. I seem to have put Mary's mind at rest regarding the safe role I am playing in this war. She'd have a fit if she knew of a few narrow escapes I have had. Poor Mary. I'm glad she is in Yorkshire now that the flying bomb attacks have commenced.

Tuesday 18 July

I believe Jerry smelt a rat last night for he was over in great force. He lit up the countryside like daylight with his flares.† If he saw anything he was too late anyway, for this morning at 0745 hrs Op Goodwood commenced with the biggest air bombardment of the war. What a prelude! 3,600 bombers of all shapes and sizes dropped 8,000 tons of bombs on SW Caen in 2 hours. I thought those planes were never going to stop.

The bombs fell so thick and fast that, from the ground, some Germans initially thought that the R.A.F. was dropping leaflets. "Men were knocked unconscious by blast, while the bomb storm raged around them; amid the continuous whistle rising to a scream of the approaching bombs, and the thunder-crack of the explosions, men heard death coming – were reprieved – heard death coming – were reprieved – heard death coming – could do nothing – and some nerves cracked; there were cases of suicide; there were cases of permanent or

---

* The man had been climbing into a jeep when a buckle on his gaiter had become caught on the trigger.
† In fact, German intelligence did know about the impending attack through air reconnaissance and agents; and the artillery barrage which followed to cover the sound of the tanks forming up simply confirmed to the Germans what was coming.

1. The author and his wife, March, 1943.

2. Father and daughter, March, 1954.

3. North Nova Scotia Highlanders going ashore at high tide, Bernières-sur-Mer, 6 June, 1944. *(G.A.Milne; National Archives of Canada; PA:122765).*

4. The beach at Bernières-sur-Mer today.

5. The author in Normandy.

6. The Chief Engineer's team open up shop. The author bottom right.

7. A Canadian Sapper
   sweeping for mines on
   the road to Caen.
   (H.G.Alkman;
   National Archives of
   Canada; PA: 132856).

8. Sappers of the 51st
   Highland Division sweeping
   for mines in Normandy.

9. The view along Juno Beach today looking from Courseulles towards Bernières-sur-Mer, which can be seen in the distance.

10. The author at work in Normandy.

11. Celebrating the capture of the radar station at Douvres-La-Deliverande.

12. The author's grandson explores the ruins of the radar station in July, 1985. Douvres-La-Deliverande can be seen in the background.

13. Canadian troops entering Caen, 10 July, 1944. *(H.G.Alkman; National Archives of Canada; PA:116510)*.

14. The Abbaye-aux-Hommes, Caen.

15. The church tower at Banville was a snipers' nest.

temporary insanity; the stunning effect temporarily incapacitated everyone. Nerves, emotions were drained; it was impossible to think. The scenery had vanished. The farms and fields had gone, wiped out. In their place was a wild moon landscape of brown craters, wreathed in the acrid smell of high explosives. Tanks caught fire; tanks were buried; men were buried; a 60–ton Tiger was blown upside down. And still the R.A.F. poured overhead, the great black-painted night-bombers roaring low to make certain of their aim." (Ibid p. 281)

The sappers erected the bridges in record time. I hope that the RAF hasn't knocked them down for the bombing seemed pretty close. After the bombing began a Victory shoot by the RA – and a Victory shoot is some shoot, when all the guns in the Corps open up simultaneously on one map reference and can plaster it from either 1 hour to two days. In this case the 'shoot' lasted some four hours.* First news to come through was that the bridges were perfect – so we were happy. 8 Corps had got all their armour across. Faubourg de Vaucelles was quite dead and at the end of the day the infantry had advanced 8 miles east to Hubert-Folie and 6 miles south to Verson. This is a jolly good show for Jerry had some good troops down that side, well positioned too. For the past fortnight we have been taking prisoners from divs that have moved down from Holland and Belgium. These moves are a very difficult operation for Jerry, for if he doesn't make them by night, then he is apt to arrive at the scene of operations minus transport. The Typhoons wreak havoc with his convoys.

Wednesday 19 July
The advance had been slowed down a little by this morning, but 8 Corps have been able to consolidate their gains. However, their original intention to 'snatch' the Falaise–Caen line will be defeated and they will have to be satisfied with what they have got. Of course we always plan a little bit more than we can do, so that in attempting to capture Falaise we do at least get a foothold on the ground in between. I don't think for a minute the army commanders thought we would capture Caen on D Day although we had planned for it in London.

* However, some of the shells from this artillery barrage fell short, killing and wounding tank crews on the start line, which caused some disorder just before the advance commenced.

In the confusion at the end of 18 July Allied commanders were hailing the day as a great success. This was picked up and expanded by newsmen and my father was obviously impressed too. A more sober tone creeps into his entry for 19 July. There were many differing views as to what had gone wrong. Some blamed Montgomery's caution. But many factors worked against total Allied success. The fact that only narrow lanes had been cleared of mines contributed to traffic jams and tanks became too strung out. The delay was exacerbated by R.A.F. cratering and heavy rain on the day did not help. There were more German defenders in the area than had been realized and not all the German guns had been knocked out. The leading armour had no infantry support, (the infantry was clearing the flanks further back) so, suffered badly in the rush to the high plateau from the surviving anti-tank defences. Certainly, by 20 and 21 July Goodwood was facing further German reinforcements, but the pressure was on the Allies to finish the job and head for Falaise, especially after the heady claims of victory made on the 18th.

Americans captured St Lô last night. This is a nasty spot cleared up and they should be able to deploy very well now. We should be in this location for at least another fortnight until the Yanks are able to swing round.

Thursday 20 July
You can't keep the 3rd Br Inf Div quiet for very long. They are supposed to be resting in the Escoville area, but I see that last night they made a very serious attack on Troarn. It went in at midnight and was made by our old friends the Royal Ulster Rifles. Troarn is a very tough spot indeed, being heavily mined and fortified; also some Tigers in hull-down positions.* The RUR have got in but it is touch and go whether or not they will hold it. Quite a surprise today. Somebody tried to bump Hitler off – may be all a rumour. Wouldn't make any difference to the war I'm sure. It's chaps like Rommel and Model who ought to be bumped off. Rommel is indeed a clever general but has made

* These monster tanks with their deadly 88mm guns and 7" thick front armour had reached and gone into action at Troarn as early as 11 July The finest armour that the Germans could offer, they were to cause the Allies a major headache. In the hull down position, it was not possible even to try the trick of bouncing shells off the ground into the weaker belly of the tank.

some glaring mistakes. His worst I think is the sacking of Rundstedt who is the one man who knows this country more than anyone else.

This was not a rumour, but the Stauffenberg Plot. The plot may have made a difference to the war had Hitler not survived. The army had planned to suppress the party (Goebbels was in fact arrested), and negotiate peace. But Rommel, who might have been able to negotiate with the British, had been out of action since 17 July when his car had been straffed. The plot did of course lead to the demise of Rommel.

Rain once more makes my trench untenable. Hope it doesn't bog down our armour, or keep the RAF out of the skies for long.

Friday 21 July
The RURs caught a cold at Troarn. The German 719 Pz Grn Div staged a counter-attack and kicked them out. They are now sitting on the outside licking their wounds. I thought they had taken rather a lot on. Last night Jerry had a good go at bombing our bridges at Ecarde – one class 40 Bailey* was severely damaged and has had to be closed pro tem. 59 Inf Div have now arrived on the scene and will eventually take up a position to the right of 2 Cdn Corps. They may have the job of clearing Tilly-sur-Seulles. There is only one way to clear that place and that is to have the map amended.

Saturday 22 July
First Canadian Army has now been formed, comprising of 1 Brit Corps and 2 Cdn Corps. We say adieu to the Second Brit Army. We have read quite a lot about the V1 and its attacks on London. We have so far thought it but a weak weapon and very vulnerable to our fighters, but today we saw our first and were surprised by the noise and the speed of this robot. I think our fighters would have a job on to catch it. It had been launched from the St. Nazaire area we think. Anyway, it kept on going right over us and eventually we watched it explode well in the German lines. 3 Cdn Div now with 2 Cdn Corps captured Maltot today and Baron yesterday. This is a very good

* A bridge that could carry 40 tons weight.

49

performance. I think that every foot of ground captured in that area is equal to 10 miles in the American sector, there is such a terrific concentration of men and material in those small villages.*

Sunday 23 July
The 49th West Riding Division came under our command today. I'm pleased to see this Div with us for they are a true blue Yorkshire Div with all my own county regiments. They also have a territorial regt called the Hallamshires. This Div spent about two years on Iceland[†] and had a thin time of it. Just yet they have been given no operational role but I think they are being kept for the 'breakout'.

Monday 24 July
2 Cdn Corps launch a heavy attack SW of Caen and as is to be expected, progress is very slow. What they have captured is good going but they have paid a heavy price for it. Their line is now Esquay – Maltot – May-sur-Orne. The latter is still very fluid. I believe 49 Div are to pass through 3 Div's positions tonight and hope to take Tilly-la-Campagne in the near future. Prisoners of war show the appearance of the Hermann Goering Panzer Div opposite the 49 Div. The Germans are really pouring in some troops just now. I wonder what the armchair critics in England are saying about our slow progress. I suppose it does look a little slow after our lightning invasion. Still, until we get time and room to stretch a bit then our progress is bound to be slow. The Germans' 'stop-block' tactics are being very well executed. But if we manage to breach his wall at any point then we'll spread all over him like a burst dam.[‡] The Americans have launched a big attack down the west side of the Cherbourg peninsula. Seems to be going very well too.

---

* The capture of Maltot was part of the continuing battle for Hill 112, and, according to the historian of the 43 Wessex Division, presented: "An appalling spectacle, the streets and fields still strewn with the dead of the Dorsets and Hampshires who had fallen on July 10th, and lay in heaps around slit trenches." (Ibid. p. 261)
† Hence their divisional flash – the Polar Bear. After the battle of Fontenay, 25 June, they earned the nickname, the 'Butcher Bears'.
‡ The beachhead was still only 15 miles deep by this stage.

Tuesday 25 July
Heavy German counter-attacks threw the Cdns out of May-sur-Orne. It is very bitter fighting down there just now and losses are great on both sides. But the highlight of the day was when the King's Own Yorkshire Light Infantry of 49 Div waded into Tilly-la-Campagne and laid about themselves with such vigour that the Hermann Goering elements were lucky to get out but a few men. This bastion was liquidated with the aid of the Crocodile, a flame-thrower used by the Assault Engineers. A very successful weapon for winkling out the Tobruk Shelters and turning Tigers in hull down positions into ovens. Once these Heinies get firmly embedded in a place they take a lot of shifting, and they have been embedding themselves for the past four years.

Wednesday 26 July
I had another 'Tour de Bridgehead' today, this time with Jack Gallon, the Chief's Humber driver. We were out to collect certain stores from 21 Army Gp dump at Sommervieu, miles behind the line. Conditions in the bridgehead are still terrible. RE and Pioneers by the thousand are working on hasty road construction but it is a losing game against all the armour that is still milling about. We have so many tanks concentrated in 'these few fields' that they just simply can't make their way to the front. Our limousine has CE well displayed and the MPs, showing due respect, clear the roads for us. On arrival at Sommervieu I was surprised and disgusted at the lazy life that these base wallahs were having. Under the shade of HQ 21 Army Group they are allowed to live a life of leisure for their staff is so enormous for the small amount of work they have to do. A 'clever' Sgt sitting in a huge marquee was receiving representatives of all the different formations enquiring after stores. He had a 'clever' remark for each one of us, much to the amusement of all the other 'stooges' sat around. To me he said, "Chief Engineer 1 Corps? Never heard of him." I told him that he had come in so late that I was surprised he had ever heard of anybody especially being so far back too. I sympathised with the difficulty he must be having when he heard all these strange names of units from the front line – I almost didn't get my stores. Whilst on this trip I took the opportunity to look up Frank. I knew he was in the 10th Beach Group with the 305 Gen Tpt Coy (*General Transport Company*) RASC and that this Beach Gp were in 102 Sub Area Beach. They are stretched from

Arromanches to Graye-sur-Mer. This was enough information for me. En route to Arromanches the convoys were so thick and heavy that we had to engage four-wheeled drive and take to the fields to avoid them, making enquiries of every MP, but an MP knows nothing outside a radius of ten yards from where he stands. Arriving at Arromanches we had a grand view of that miraculous feat of the Royal Navy – Op Mulberry. Op Mulberry entailed the construction, of iron, concrete and steel, of a huge floating dock stretching some two miles out to sea, for our ships carrying all the necessities of war to supply a vast army, to unload upon. In my wildest dreams I never pictured a scene like this. The beaches of Normandy were transformed overnight into a miniature Southampton, for this dock floated and was towed over by the Navy, under most difficult circumstances in rough seas, anchored at Arromanches and almost immediately our ships were able to unload straight on to waiting transport. I saw the biggest concentration of AA in this war for the defence of this masterpiece. Frank was finally located 'in a field' and it was good to see him. He looked well and very fit. We talked and laughed for a couple of hours.

Thursday 27 July
The American push is now getting under way and they will soon be within striking distance of Avranches. Jerry will carefully have to watch his left flank or the Americans will be squeezing through. It's only very thinly held out there. 49 Div are severely punishing the 2 SS Pz Div and are gathering in quite a harvest of prisoners. Rumours have it that wounded Hitler Jugend (fanatics) volunteer to have a booby trap placed under them as they lie beside the road. This will make things awkward for our RAMC. Best thing to do is leave them alone.

Friday 28 July
We had a heluva night. I was glad when I saw the dawn break. I was on duty in the Vic and the blasted Luftwaffe were over all night. The vehicle simply reared as the bombs came down and shrapnel rattled on the top from our AA. He is still thinking he can put our Ranville bridges out of action. I felt rough this morning. I saw Caen today for the first time, that is I entered it. I knew it was bad from what the Chief Engineer had told us, but it has to be seen to be believed. It is impossible to recognize or even to imagine the shape of this city – there are no roads or streets

– just all rubble, black rubble, and the stench is sickening. Somewhere in those ruins lay 3,000 bodies.

The city presented a desolate sight. The following description appeared in Pegasus Goes to it, *the newssheet of the 6th Airborne Division: "The first thing that strikes you is the signs of the grim struggles our chaps must have had before taking the city: cratered roads, burnt-out tanks, ruined houses, and the pathetic sight of once-treasured personal possessions of a peaceful community now blasted and scattered by the unjust hand of war – clothes, pictures, furniture, kids' toys, and all the little things which make 'home' . . . Some streets are almost untouched except for cracked and broken windows; but you only have to turn the corner to find many a mountain of ruins where, no doubt, many a peaceful civilian lies buried in a grave as honourable as any soldier's. The clean, lovely smell of wet fields; the sickening stench of burnt-out ruins; the calm, normal behaviour of desperately tired civilians; the charred remains of a dead Nazi lying in the wreckage of his tank up a quiet side-street; tired but cheerful Tommies, all looking about eighteen, teaching their new friends English and learning French with the help of cigarettes, sweets, and much good humour; old women washing the salvaged bits and pieces of their household linen in the gardens of their ruined homes; Frenchmen finding a bottle of cider in the ruins of their homes and offering it to our chaps – all these odd, disturbing contrasts are to be seen in every street still recognisable as a street." (Quoted in R.N. Gale, Op. cit. p. 121)*

Even though their city is finished the inhabitants seemed cheerful when I spoke to them. They said that the SW of the city was not quite so bad. I don't know, I didn't get that far. The Maquis have already arrested the Mayor and collaborators – the Mayor is to be shot tomorrow.

Saturday 29 July
Although we get plenty of food I don't think it is doing us much good. We get very little variety – only stew followed by rice. Some of the chaps are having a little stomach trouble. 1 Corps front is very stable just now and all our divs are keeping quiet. 1 Corps is now the hinge of all 21 Army Gp and the Americans too. On us they will swing someday towards Paris. But when I come to look at the map and see what a little bit we hold and what a huge country France is I sometimes think that we are in for another

100 Years War. The Germans are a very stubborn race. They are, after all, professional soldiers. We are still but amateurs at the game. Only our weight of arms and air superiority have put us where we are today. German casualties are almost double ours just now.

Chapter Five

The Break Out

By the end of July two million Allied and German troops were battling it out in a tiny triangle of Normandy from Caen to Avranches to Cherbourg. While the British and Canadians held the bulk of the German armour at Caen, the American plan was to break out to the Brittany ports, then, fed by supplies and reinforcements through those ports, to swing round on the Caen pivot and push the Germans back to the Seine.

When the German front at Avranches in the U.S. sector began to crumble, Montgomery seized the opportunity to strike in the centre of the British–American line at Caumont (fifty miles from Caen), where the British and American forces met. The idea was that here, the twin British–American thrust would split, the Americans wheeling round to the right to Brittany, the British to the left. So, the bulk of the British forces were switched rapidly to this sector, with 8 Corps, 30 Corps, and various armoured brigades making up the main attack.

On 30 July, the attack went in and a six-mile corridor was created by 11th Armoured Division and 15th Scottish Division. But their left flank was dominated by the German-held Mont Pincon (Normandy's "Little Switzerland"), which the Germans had to hold if their forces were not to be cut off and surrounded. A bridge over the River Souleuvre was captured intact on 31 July, which allowed the Allies to fan out into the bocage country beyond. The Germans switched troops and armour from Hill 112 (south-west Caen) to Vire on 1 August, to check this burst in the dam and to hold their lines of communication along the Mont Pincon Ridge. After days of fierce fighting by infantry against strongly held positions on the mountain, Mont Pincon was eventually captured on 6–7 August.

This was followed by the battle to establish a bridgehead across the River Orne. On 4 August the 6th North Staffords of 59th Division had *captured Villers-Bocage. On 6–7 August they crossed a bridge hastily erected by Royal Engineers sappers across the Orne. The bridgehead was held in the next few days in the face of a fierce German counter-attack (leading to 90% casualties in some rifle companies), largely due to the superior fire-power of the artillery.*

Sunday 30 July

8 Corps and 30 Corps packing practically all armoured divs, 7 Armd, 11 Armd, 79 Armd – 43 Wessex, 53 Welch and 15 Scottish divisions have been concentrating on the Americans' left and today launched a massive attack, centreing on Balleroy, on Caumont. This is going to be tough going before it even begins and interesting too. 7 Armd are opposed by their old rival 21 Panzer Div.* 2 Panzer Lehr are there too, backed up by a lot of non-descript infantry divs. The Germans have the position but we have the RAF and fine weather. Jerry's long-range guns got a bead on our HQ once more last night. He missed, but he made our trenches feel cosy.

Monday 31 July

What news greeted us this morning – the whole HQ is all agog. The miracle has happened. We are breaking out. Good old 30 Corps and 8 Corps too, under the personal direction of General Montgomery swamped the German positions and, practically running behind our aircraft liquidated the Caumont bastion and just now are reforming 11 miles past it. What an advance! I can imagine the flap in Jerry's 2nd echelon as our infantry overran his base wallahs – captured a couple of Lt Generals too. I don't know who they are yet. The Americans also dashed forward and occu-pied Avranches. This was all very good news and put us in great spirits, but one other item that I regret to report was the death of our Lt Col McDowell. He was on one of his airfields when an ammunition truck was straffed and set on fire. There were many aircraft in the vicinity and that truck had to be moved. He drove to it in a jeep and attempted to fasten a tow rope but he was too late and the whole wagon went up. He was a perfect gentleman and he and I got on very well together indeed.†

---

* They had already met in battle, 12–15 June.
† Lt. Col. William James McDowell had only been posted to the 16th Airfield Construction Group R.E. on 23 July. Aged 36, he had already

Tuesday 1 August
The Germans are packing a little more weight in on our front just now and are trying to dislodge us. 49 Div are very fresh still and Jerry's efforts are in vain. We stand like a rock now. The Boche's fingers are getting burnt. We've got to hang on anyway for 30 and 8, although hardly reformed, are pushing on again and the Americans had even got into the Brest Peninsula. A French farmer gave us a bottle of Calvados today. This is the genuine fire water if ever there was one. I got horribly drunk and slept from dinner-time until 11pm, then on duty with a most terrible headache.

Wednesday 2 August
Americans today entered Rennes. Their swift-moving convoys nosed their way through the German defence lines and snatched this town before a serious counter-attack could be got under way. British Second Army under Gen Dempsey pushed on another 2 miles south of Caumont. Everything is now going according to the planning early this year and if the weather holds good I can foresee a huge German collapse in the near future.

Thursday 3 August
A few hours free so I walked in to La Deliverande. This place is becoming impossible and is a bad bottleneck for our convoys. Lines of tanks and lorries wait hours on the roads trying to nose their way to the front. I saw a smashing bicycle and of course I had to examine it closely. Its owner was none other than the renowned Tribouillard of Tour de France fame. We talked cycling for two hours and the French flew so thick and fast that I had to lapse into broad Yorkshire to keep my end up. Our talk ended with me getting an invitation to his wedding at Cazelle and also a challenge to a hill climb race. I craftily arranged that the date of this event would be a fortnight after the date of the wedding!* I think of all the strongpoints in Normandy Villers-Bocage has proved to be the worst. Poor 59 Div has hurled attack after attack

---

won the D.S.O. in the Middle East, as reported in the *London Gazette*, 13 January, 1944. He is buried in Bayeux War Cemetery.
* When the war broke out my father's career as a racing cyclist (hill climb specialist) was just beginning to blossom. I do not think that the Tribouillard challenge ever materialized, but his meeting with the great man, and later with Jan Pijnenburg in Holland, were highlights of my father's time in Europe.

on this village and they have always got the worst of it. The country around this place is very wooded and our recce planes cannot get the information of Jerry's dispositions. Actually I think we've never given either Villers-Bocage or Evrecy a big enough attack to carry the day, but we will have to do soon.

Friday 4 August
The Americans are certainly losing no time in their brilliant advance across the Brest Peninsula. I think that their army is the most mobile in the world. They are now on the outskirts of St. Nazaire. They departed Rennes in three columns, one wheeling right and heading for Brest itself, one for St Nazaire and the other making for Nantes. It is this latter thrust that is of the most importance, for this, I think will be the beginning of the big 'wheel-round'.

Saturday 5 August
Nice news this morning (after another bombfire last night). 59 Div with elements of 79 Armd Div effected huge slaughter on the Germans in Villers-Bocage and now hold the remains of that village for good an' all. Evrecy too has gone the same way, but I'm not quite certain of its captors yet. I understand that a Victory shoot was necessary to finally erase them.

Chapter Six

Totalise, Tallulah and Tractable – the Cauldron of Falaise

By 7 August the Americans were pushing southwards towards Angers and eastwards to Le Mans, and the possibility of an envelopment of the German army in Normandy (with the British and Canadians in the north) became very real. Meanwhile, Hitler was still ordering his generals to push westwards to counter-attack the Americans, thereby driving his forces deeper and deeper into the pocket. Montgomery saw his opportunity to trap the German Seventh Army and seal the enemy's escape by pushing the Canadians and British towards Falaise and Argentan to meet up with the Americans coming up from the south.

Montgomery's plan was for British, Canadian and Polish troops to race down a corridor from Caen to Falaise, with air attacks on either flank. This first phase from 7 to 11 August, known as Operation Totalise (or 'down the corridor' to the troops), would involve four columns of armour and armoured infantry charging south to Falaise by night, covered by a thousand-bomber raid on the flanks. They had to try to break through to the rear of the German lines without stopping. This was to be followed the next day by the advance of two more armoured divisions (fresh troops of the 4th Canadian and the 1st Polish), also supported by carpet bombing on the flanks, who would finish off the stunned German front line.

The first wave of the night of 7–8 August was successful, but the daylight attack on the 8th got off to a bad start. Units of Canadians, Poles and the 51 (H) Division were bombed in error on the start line by the U.S. Eighth Air Force. There were over 300 casualties, of whom 65 were killed. One Canadian unit displayed its frustration by opening fire on the U.S. bombers. The newcomers were wary and inexperienced and so did not push on as fast as was hoped, and by 10 August, the attack had stalled only half way to Falaise, with heavy casualties.

Another full set-piece attack was needed. Codenamed Operation Tallulah, the name was changed on 13 August to Tractable because of difficulties with the spelling and pronunciation of the original! On 14 August the 3rd Canadian Infantry Division, 4th and 79th Armoured Divisions charged down the corridor in two waves – 160 tanks in the first wave, and 90 in the second, with armoured infantry in 'kangaroos'. The object was to attack impregnable anti-tank emplacements before Falaise, especially in the region of Quesnay Woods. The attack, in broad daylight, was masked by an artificial smoke screen, and the tank and carrier drivers were ordered to follow the sun, the only thing they could make out in this man-made fog. There was a simultaneous bombing attack on the flanks which led to yet another tragedy. Seventy-seven planes of Bomber Command, off target, bombed Allied troops with serious results. There were many hundreds of casualties. More than 150 were killed. The advance of 14 August down a smoking, blind corridor against formidable anti-tank defences became known as the 'mad charge' to the troops, but seven miles were covered in two days.

Falaise was not completely taken until August 16th and the Canadians and British pushed on to finally seal the pocket, with the village of St Lambert at the centre, by 21 August. While all this was going on, there was a mad rush by German troops to escape. Many surrendered, but others fought with great tenacity, and the pocket was the scene of great slaughter and devastation. French civilians were caught up in the nightmare also. At the end of it all, the scene was like something from Dante. The stench of death in the heat of August was so powerful, that pilots in observation planes overhead recoiled at the smell and those on the ground, left with the task of mopping up, had to wear gas masks. The pocket was finally cleared by the end of August, but half the German army had made its escape. Falaise was not the Stalingrad that the Allies had hoped for.

Sunday 6 August

Corps HQ today moved to Biéville and harboured in the grounds of an ancient château. This château is a horrible mess. It once housed the HQ of our opposite number, 89 German Corps HQ, but alas the Typhoons got to know about it and now 89 Corps are advertising for a new HQ. As a matter of fact the whole German staff are still in the château somewhere. It is a sickening location, and in this hot weather the stench is horrible. We've decided after all that we *are* going to have Falaise and Op Totalise is now commencing. 49 Div have got their chance and are slogging their way down the Caen–Falaise main road, 2 Cdn Corps are keeping up with them, 3 Br are there too and 51st Highland and bags of armour, including 5 Aslt Regt RE. Every foot of the way is mined and booby trapped, but we're going to Falaise for I think we have a date with the Yanks in that district.

Monday 7 August
The smell of dead men and cattle forced us to leave Biéville and we moved over the River Orne to Giberville. As we moved into an orchard a RA Regt moved out with their 5.5s. I didn't like the look of this place. Troarn was too close as well. We were just putting the finishing touches to our tents, it was practically dark, although 12 midnight, when a shrill long-drawn-out whistle announced the arrival of the first shell, bullseye too. By now we know exactly what to do in such circumstances. We kept low. A second and a third shell followed, then more and more. The shrapnel moaned over our heads, but we were able to time the interval between these shells and in turn we dashed for our slit trenches, which is the first thing a soldier makes in a new location, if he wants to live. I made my dash during a lull. I couldn't see by now, but I knew where safety lay. I didn't know though what lay in between. I seemed to be falling for quite some time before I eventually crashed into the bottom of a pit containing everything that the RA boys had no use for. A dud 5.5 dug savagely into my knee and I felt sick. The warm blood trickled down my leg. I heard a singing noise in my ears. I awoke next morning frozen almost stiff. My leg refused to move and I was scared lest it was broken, but as I had been sitting on it all night, it couldn't be expected to operate at a minute's notice. I dragged myself out of this filthy place and with the aid of a friend saw the MO. He washed a nasty wound, and said it would be OK.* Our cooks' wagon had received a direct hit and the signals also announced casualties. We ate apples for breakfast, licked our wounds and laughed at each other's experiences.

* In fact, it was not O.K. By the end of the war he was having operations to remove splinters of shrapnel.

But this afternoon we got out of the joint and moved a little nearer Caen. The heat is becoming almost unbearable and we work very scantily dressed. Our new location is quite near to the famous Colombelles factory. What a jumbled heap it is now – 12,000 bombs did this, plus the Navy, plus a few RA Victory shoots. A well known smell near our cookhouse revealed the presence of an SS man. He had long since given his life for the Fatherland.

Tuesday 8 August
It's a case of every man to the wheel now, for big things are happening and history is being made every minute. The Americans have swung round, according to plan, and with a brilliant stroke Gen Patton has captured Nantes, Angers and Le Mans thus getting right behind our common enemy. Armies of 21 Army Gp are smashing their way towards Falaise in what must be some of the bitterest fighting of the war. We're putting all we have into this big push and the Hun is doing likewise. The cream of the German army is slowly but surely being caught in a huge pocket. This is Montgomery's master stroke, which, if successful, may end the war this year. I will never forget these days, the heat, the dust and the days that last till midnight – and most of all I will never forget the mosquitoes. These horrible pests are torturing us day and night. This valley of the Orne is the ideal breeding ground, and they can get as much blood as they require. In our trenches at night time we sleep fully clothed with a gas cape around our heads. The heat is terrific and we bathe in sweat, but the 'mozzies' find a way in and should you swipe one on your neck you will find a patch of blood where you squash it, for these insects feed well on the dead men on the battlefield.

Wednesday 9 August
Canadians announce that they are within 5 miles of Falaise – good for Cdns. Their 4 Cdn Armd Div has surely punished the 2 Panzer Div. The Americans made a sad mistake today when they bombed our own troops in Colombelles factory. One Fortress jettisoned its bombs and the others thought they were on the target. Our lads got the full blast from 300 bombers that was meant to pave a way to Falaise – I felt sick as I watched this happen. (*See Appendix 2*) We are working like madmen now and must only sleep when a lull occurs. There is a slight touch of dysentery in

our camp. The 'mozzies' have 'got' our food, or perhaps it is the flies.* All day long the RA barrage never ceases, the bombers are doing relay work and our infantry and sappers creep slowly towards Falaise.

Thursday 10 August
The Americans are approaching Argentan having already captured Alençon last night. They are right behind the enemy now and he doesn't know which way to turn. He dare not ease up against the British for a minute or else we would 'steam roller' him. The shimmering heat must be terrible for our tank men. Five of our chaps are sick with dysentery. I've given up all hope of ever sleeping again, but I'm terribly happy at the trend of events. Rumour has it that Rommel has been killed by one of our Typhoons – hope so.† Even though our mail is once more still looking for us, I don't worry.

Friday 11 August
In a jeep I went to Bretteville-sur-Odon and found the father and mother of René Ledésert, a professor at Eton College with whom I had correspondence whilst at Douvres. Their beautiful house had been demolished by our friends the SS as they said it would be turned into a strong point by the British thus making it more difficult for the SS to retake when they returned. What a hope.

René Ledésert – languages teacher at Eton and co-editor with his wife of Harrap's Standard French-English Dictionary. By a strange coincidence, I read the announcement of his death in the Telegraph *in November, 1984. I wrote to his widow, explaining that my father had met the Ledésert family during the Invasion, and received a most interesting letter from her in return. It seems that Mme Ledésert, the*

---

* The Royal Signals, among others, were having the same trouble: "Mild form of dysentery sweeping through the Unit. Consultation with M.O. confirmed no cause for anxiety. Mosquitoes, flies and wasps in new area very severe. A blitz arranged on all refuse and salvage in an attempt to reduce infection." (War Diary C.R.E. 1st Corps Signals Coy: WO 171/270, 11 Aug, 1944.)
† In fact Rommel's car had been straffed by a fighter-bomber on 17 July and he had been very seriously injured. Perhaps the story of his death came out now because it more or less coincided with the news that Hitler had purged his enemies, but the circumstances of his death became confused amid rumour. He committed suicide in October, 1944.

mother of René, had been evacuated from Caen to Douvres. When the British troops arrived, she stood at the roadside asking them, "Parlez-vous Français? Parlez-vous Français?" My father did, and stopped to help. He was able to get word back to René in England that his family had survived the occupation. This was the first news he had had since the German invasion in 1940. A long correspondence and exchange of gifts followed. I still have the inscribed French dictionary from René Ledésert, that my father passed to me when I won my scholarship to grammar school. René also sent my father a German dictionary, so he must have had confidence in the outcome of the Invasion.

As a result of our correspondence I went to visit the Ledéserts in Bretteville (a suburb of Caen) in 1985, now living in a house built on the site of their destroyed home. We enjoyed a wonderful meal with the family and then went together to watch the 14 July fireworks in Caen. The father of the family, André, was 99 years old. He clearly remembered Corporal Womack, and it made the hairs on my arms stand up to hear this still dapper Frenchman describe my father as 'a fine young Englishman'".

The whole countryside that I saw was a complete shambles. This must be scorched earth. Refugees by the thousand are pouring from Falaise. Troops with faces like leather and looking very tired are pushing on to the 'gap'. We've got Jerry this time and he will have a terrible job to withdraw his troops.

Saturday 12 August
The Americans have got Argentan. This is great news but they have now been blocked by two Panzer divs and I doubt if they will get much further. Anyway, part of Gen Patton's force is mysteriously nosing its way along the Paris road and was last heard of as far as Chartres. The Cdns have launched two major attacks on Falaise but both have failed. Many Cdns lost their lives in these operations. Our 51st and 49th Divs are both there; 7 Armd Div entered Thury Harcourt today. But the action which has put the Germans more in a mess was when they tried to suddenly push through to Avranches and thus cut the Americans' supply lines. They gained some 10 miles before our Typhoons came along and knocked out 80 Tigers. A crafty move by the RAF some 4 hours later when the Typhoons again went in and knocked out the tank transporters Jerry sent in to salvage his lost 80. This has just about put the Boche in the cart good and proper. He has

got some 20 Divs in this pocket – the finest Divs in his army, about 150,000 men and equipment which he can ill afford to lose.

Sunday 13 August
The British Second Army are now bringing pressure to bear on the gap. The slaughter amongst the Germans is terrible; they won't surrender although they are being subjected to Victory shoots and bombing, day and night. They are so concentrated now that their tanks have no room to deploy and their men are tumbling over each other. They are still holding Falaise, but after tomorrow there will no longer be a Falaise, for tomorrow sees the start of Op Tallulah, which deletes this city from the map of France. Maj Bays our SO II (Ops) had to be taken to hospital with dysentery today. We now have 8 men suffering from this complaint in our branch alone, although 75% of the whole HQ has it. We have been issued with anti-mosquito ointment but the mosquitoes like it and unless it is laid on at least 1" thick they'll still get you. I look as though I have the measles from all the bites.*

Monday 14 August
51st Highland Div wanted so badly to capture Falaise during Op Tallulah that they got over the bomb line and our Lancasters and Stirlings bombed them for 1½ hours, our Typhoons and Spitfires straffed their convoys and inflicted heavy casualties. This is quite understandable just now for there is a terrible mix-up around Falaise. I feel sorry for the old 51st though, for they are a grand div and have done noble work since D + 3. (*See Appendix 2*) Another operation to capture Falaise is planned, this time Op Tractable and Gen Crerar himself has written and told us we *must* get Falaise at all costs.† We were shelled again today, but they were only inners and we suffered no casualties.

---

* In the *Yorkshire Pud*, a newssheet published at frequent intervals for the 7th Bn. the Duke of Wellington's Regt it is reported that "the Battalion was attacked by hordes of mosquitoes which made life in the slit trench very uncomfortable and, although the medical services issued various creams and potions, as well as nets, the mosquitoes were always there causing not a little discomfort."
† "Hit him first, hit him hard, and keep on hitting. We can contribute in a major degree to speed Allied victory by our action." Gen Crerar's message to the troops taking part in Tractable, 14 August, 1944.

Tuesday 15 August

Got it this time OK, but we had to practically knock every brick in Falaise to do it, down to the ground. Jerry knows he has 'had it' in the gap now as it is only 12 miles wide and we and the Americans can bring our artillery to bear on all the escape roads. He's running the gauntlet too and maybe at night he manages to extricate a chosen few. He's making no attempt to save the Wehrmacht though.* There was another landing this morning from Italy onto the south coast of France between Nice and Marseilles. There is very little news yet, but this is a good stroke. We are far too engrossed in our own work to notice what is going on around us. The mosquitoes have taken two more of our staff and this is now putting me on duty every night, though I also have slight symptoms. The mosquitoes delight in catching us on the latrines. They are enough to drive a man mad. Everything is covered in a powdery dust and it is as hot as hell all the time. Capt Stewart and I thought we'd had it last night when Jerry came over and bombed all round us. We nearly had too, when we came to look where we sheltered after running from the Vic. We dashed to a trench that was full of boxes and literally hurled them away so that we could crouch down. This morning we looked at the boxes, carelessly left by the RA, and they contained high explosive charges!

Wednesday 16 August

Well the slaughter in the gap is going along nicely. Our armies are sat all around its rim which is roughly Falaise – Flers – Barenten – Mayenne – Pré – Argentan and are hosing the enemy with bullets and shells. He is trying desperately to break out, but is is impossible. This is Montgomery's master stroke of the war, and probably the end of the German army. We've got 2 Pz Lehr, 21 SS Pz, 879, 880, 881 Pz Grenadiers, Hitler Jugend, Hermann Goering and at least 10 divs of the Wehrmacht. 1 Corps have now taken under command one of the best divs in the British army – the 7th Armoured Division. Highlight of the day has been made by the 51st Div who have suddenly wheeled away from the gap and before you could say 'knife' were over the River Dives and well on their way to Lisieux. They covered 35 miles in one day.

* While many of the SS were rushing back to defend Germany, the Wehrmacht was left to its fate in the pocket.

Thursday 17 August
The gap is now closed and it is all over bar the shouting. It was a long hard fight and it cost us some good men but the prize is terrific. We've caught enough squareheads to start another war. They're throwing their hands up now, but this doesn't make much difference to the Cdns. They are remembering their 20 comrades who were murdered by the men they are now capturing – did I say capturing? We're off once more on the next stage of the annihilation of the Teutonic thuggery and this time Corps HQ stays at Quatre Puis. Lisieux and the Seine is our objective. The death and destruction of an army trying to escape litters the roads along which we passed today. Cagny and Vimont were both German graveyards; hundreds of horses and carts and dead Germans were thrown into the ditches and the smell was poison. We've got 51, 49 and 7 Armd in the chase now. Below us, but parallel, 2 Cdn Corps are galloping forward, whilst Gen Patton is reported but 28 miles from Paris. What news. I am sure we are all drunk with victory – the war will be over very soon. Falaise is surely the end of Jerry.

The closing of the Gap was not the end of the matter and the Allies were hard pressed to prevent fleeing Germans from breaking through at different points. The centre point was St Lambert, the scene of bitter fighting and through which the Germans were pouring. As late as 21 August they were still breaking through. Meanwhile, the Germans outside the cauldron were attacking those trying to keep the Gap closed, from the East. The cleaning up of the pocket went on through the last week of August, by which time, 10,000 had been killed and 40,000 taken prisoner, but 50,000 had escaped.

A later edition of the Yorkshire Pud *reported "A month afterwards, Montgomery told us: 'It wasn't a pocket. It was a bottle. With the Germans inside trying to push out the cork and us pushing it back again. Eventually it was firmly stoppered and hundreds of thousands of the once proud Seventh Army were captured or killed.'" (Op. cit. p. 10) But Lt Walter Horne said that Montgomery kept easing the cork out of the bottle to let a few spill out, and then sending in the R.A.F. to finish them off. Jan Derych with the Polish Armoured Division said that so many Germans were breaking through that it was more like a colander than a bottle.*

Friday 18 August
A sweepstake has been organised on the date the war will end. At

100 francs a time we should have a nice pick-up if we win. October seems to be the most favoured month. I chose the 15th and was called a pessimist. I just daren't build up. Thoughts of the war ending and my coming out of it whole sound too good.* I long to be back in England in my own home with Mary and the baby. But right now we are working our heads off getting enough bridging material up to put an army across the Risle. Jerry got our range again. I think our wireless must have been a little careless and he knows our location. The shells whined over soon after our arrival at Quatre Puis, but now he is getting better on his mark. Brig Manners-Smith the CCRA (*Commander Corps, Royal Artillery*) will personally deal with the said Heinie guns. Counter bombardment will take place tonight. 4 AGRA are doing the job and they usually do a job well. Quatre Puis is situated in the Dives valley and the mosquitoes are so well concentrated here that Q Branch had to indent immediately to England for anti-mosquito nets, and so now we work all day with trimmings on. So far the nets have beaten the mosquitoes but they are still trying and they get us at meal times. Maj Bays returned today looking a bit wan. He said that they had taken everything away from him except his will to live.

Saturday 19 August
Today I was sent to a rest camp for about 12 hours. This is the first break I have had since England and I didn't know how tired I was until I got there. The Camp, situated at Lion-sur-Mer, was back near where we landed. It is a huge château and is staffed by French ladies and an elderly English Major. They were very good to us and I felt horribly dirty in this place, so spick and span. The first thing I did was to have a lovely hot bath. I don't know whether I was dirty or whether it was sunburn, but I seemed to be of rather a dark hue. After the bath I lounged in a wicker chair on the verandah and slept solidly until I was awakened by a sweet feminine voice, dinner was ready – Gosh! Fresh rations. I ate like a wolf and enjoyed that meal immensely, then back to sleep. In the evening there was a little concert which was quite good and at 9pm the wagon arrived to take us from this little heaven back to the war. To the incessant barrages, the roaring tanks, the bombing, the shooting and sickening desolation of a ruined

---

* A stark contrast with his attitude of 5 June – ". . . of course nothing will happen to me."

country. I felt a little fed up today as I returned. Perhaps it would have been better if I had never had the day out. It was interesting as we drove back on this hot summer evening. It was plain to see where the war had been, just like some giant slug leaving in its wake absolute and utter destruction. As we crossed the Orne at our own Ranville bridges I wondered at the amount of work they had done since D + 4 when they had been completed by our own Corps Troops RE. Then, as the noise of the guns grew stronger, we knew we were back once more. We passed through the lines of the 'heavies' and in the distant country could be seen the shelling of Lisieux.

The constant movement back and forth between war and rest, imminent danger and comparative safety, never failed to strike me as I read through the War Diaries. For instance, the Régiment de la Chaudière moved from Soliers and Four (south of Caen) to Basly for a rest on 31 July. They arrived at 0500 hours. Diary entry: "The regiment did not register any loss on arrival despite our departure being marked by the strongest concentration of artillery that we had ever witnessed. At one moment, about 200 German shells landed in 30 seconds." The very next entry reads: "1900 hrs. Bingo in the school at Basly". (Op. cit., 31 July, 1944)

Chapter Seven

The Pursuit to the Seine and the Freeing of the Channel Ports

For the Allies, the next phase of the battle in the west involved making good their bases for the winter, so their strength could be built up and the final knock-out blow delivered. The German High Command meanwhile had decided to withdraw from France and Belgium, and to retire to defensive positions in Holland in order to recover.

Before the opening of the 'second front', all the bridges on the River Seine between Paris and the sea had been destroyed by Allied air attack, to make it difficult for the Germans to reinforce the region. This had worked in the Allies' favour until they broke out of Normandy and dashed to the Seine, when the river became a barrier to their own progress. The surviving units of the German army retreated at high speed across the Seine, by ferry or pontoon, during the final week of August. The Allies, hot on their heels, were across the river in the last days of August and early September.

Hitler had refused permission for a defensive line on the Somme, so the Germans fell back to the next major water obstacle, the Meuse (Maas) and the Scheldt in eastern France and central Belgium. The Allies, in pursuit, were hampered by a shortage of fuel and supplies as their lines of communication became strung out. The Germans, hoping to deny access to the Channel ports to the Allies, left garrisons in the larger harbour towns. The First Canadian Army (including the 49th and 51st Highland Divisions) was given the task of opening up the ports of Le Havre, Boulogne, Calais, Ostend and Dieppe (where an old score had to be settled).

By 15 September Luxembourg had been liberated, the Americans were on the line of the Meuse, and the British were at Brussels, Antwerp and Maastricht. In order to thrust the Allied advance into the German Plain, Montgomery planned an air-ground attack across the Rhine. Advance airborne units were to seize vital bridges across the Rhine, paving the way for an armoured attack by ground forces. Operation Market Garden was launched on 17 September. "Market", the seizure of the Eindhoven and Nijmegen bridges by American airborne divisions went according to plan, but "Garden", in which the 1st British Airborne Division was to secure the bridge at Arnhem was a tragic failure. The British met fierce resistance from the 9th and 10th SS Panzer Divisions and ground forces could not reach Arnhem in time to save the Airborne force. They had to abandon Arnhem after 25 September.

While the British had been side-tracked by Arnhem, the Germans had been free to strengthen the defences of the Scheldt, thus denying the Allies access to the facilities of Antwerp.

Sunday 20 August

A surprise change in the weather. It's simply teeming with rain – this might kill the 'mozzies'. The Americans have reached the Seine below Paris. Our 6 Airborne Div with under their command Belgian and Dutch contingents have formed a light infantry div and already have entered Troarn and are swiftly making their way along the coast clearing up Cabourg, Deauville, and are approaching Honfleur. The Germans are going to try and hold us at Lisieux for as long as possible to get the remnants of their broken army back across the Seine. This is going to be difficult as the RAF have blown all the bridges. They might try ferrying under cover of darkness. Anyway 2 Cdn Corps are almost to the Seine already.

Monday 21 August

The army that landed in the south of France is now known as the 7th Army and is made up of American and British elements. They captured Toulon yesterday. Our 7 Armd Div are now but 3 miles from Lisieux. The heavy rains have bogged them down a little, and Jerry is indeed lucky to get this breather, but all divs are now in for the kill. This German army must not escape, it MUST be annihilated. Only excellent organisation on the enemy's part has managed to hold these remnants together till now. Patton approaches Paris. 6 Airborne still pushing on. 51st successfully bridge the Risle at Pont Audemer. The Maquis claim to have liberated this town. It is difficult to keep a clear picture just now for things are moving very fast. No sooner do we receive a situation report than it is out of date and superseded by another.

Tuesday 22 August
1 mile to go and 7 Armd have done it. Lisieux is beginning to crumble and with the loss of that the army of the super race can 'write home for more stamps', because they will never get across the Seine. 2 Cdn Corps are almost at the Seine but well on our right. A Victory shoot tonight on Lisieux. If the Germans try to pin the rap on us for destroying this town, we won't wear it, for ever since they got in they have been doing demolitions on all major buildings in order to stop up the roads. We will get our supplies up a little quicker now for we have got 12 bridges across the River Touques.

Wednesday 23 August
The Victory shoot did the trick OK and 7 Armd moved in this morning. The Boche still showed fight, however, and I think that our Shermans and Churchills ran foul of some Tigers in hull-down positions. There were quite a number of prisoners; they looked in a bad way. Most of them had beards, some were only about 17 years old, remnants of the Hitler Jugend I should imagine. Very few had a pair of good boots to their feet. The German is a tough soldier though, we all admit that. He fights like a fanatic, which we Englishmen fail to understand.

Hans Braun of a German tank unit said: "Often we were accused of fighting fanatically, but we had long since learned the lesson, that one thing alone counts in war; to fire first, by a fraction of a second, and kill; or otherwise be killed oneself. Apart from that, in this sixth year of the war, we Germans knew what was in store for us. But because we were in reality defending our homeland, our parents, our wives and children, who had already suffered unspeakably from the attacks of the enemy night-bombers, we were determined, if necessary, to fall by our guns before we would let the enemy advance a step farther." (Quoted in McKee, Op. cit., p. 114)

The HQ moved up to Lisieux to a little place called La Motte. On arriving there we heard the astounding news that Paris had fallen and that the French Div with the American army had entered and that but for a little street fighting they'd got the place, captured first of all by the FFI.

Thursday 24 August
The 7th Army in the south are making grand progress and followed up yesterday's capture of Toulon by capturing Marseilles also. The Germans in Paris asked for an armistice and then – bad lads – they violated their terms and so heavy street fighting has broken out in the metropolis. I'm sure now that the war will collapse before very long – we will all be in 'civvy street' by Christmas. Don't think that they will send us D Day boys to the Far East. I wonder if we will have to go up through Belgium and Holland. Shouldn't think this would be necessary. Jerry has withdrawn his forces from there. I suppose we will make for the German frontier. When we arrive there he will pack up, for they will never fight long on their own soil. They wouldn't have that in the last war. 50 Div of 30 Corps are mighty close to the Seine now. They captured Evreux yesterday and are inflicting terrible losses on the enemy.

Friday 25 August
Paris has been about cleared now and the French div has everything under control. Gen de Gaulle is in command and he almost lost his life at the hands of a sniper. Roumania has seen sense and 'jacked up'. Won't be long now. That's one less anyway. 50 Div reached the Seine this morning and 30 Corps are asking us for bridging material. They'll get it too, like h——. Why didn't they foresee this advance and get all their bridging equipment on wheels like we had to do? We'll be on the Seine ourselves in a few days. I was in Lisieux this morning. What a sight. Another Caen it seems, although miraculously the 'basilique' hasn't suffered much harm. Five airmen came into our lines this morning. They've been hidden by the French since February of this year. They looked very fit and well and were dressed as French peasants. There are three hundred dead horses in the fields approaching Lisieux, killed by our aircraft and dumped there by the pioneers for eventual burning. The Germans use mostly horse-drawn transport, they have no petrol.

Saturday 26 August
We push on a little further – 20 miles – and Corps HQ set up shop at another La Motte. Things seem a little more peaceful just now

for the artillery cannot keep up with this headlong rush for the Seine. We have to step very warily though for these approaches are heavily mined but the Germans laid them hastily and our sappers can pick them up quickly. Brig Campbell our CE had a very narrow squeak today. He went up to the Risle to look at a bridging site he had in mind, went through the German lines and got in an ambush. He and his driver lay in a ditch and were fired on by a machine gun. He tore up his maps and shot his way out of the jam with his revolver, killed the machine gunner and managed to escape. Some more Calvados, but this time only a little, but a lot of the boys were zig-zag on it.

Sunday 27 August
49 Div are first over the Risle and in full headlong dash for the Seine. 1 Corps will NOT bridge the Seine but will cross on 2 Cdn Corps bridges at Elbeuf which was captured yesterday and bridged today. I believe the Cdn sappers have set up a new world's record with the Bailey at this crossing.

*The 90th Field Company, R.E. came under the command of the 2nd Canadian Corps. They described the bridging of the Seine at Elbeuf thus: "Company moved overnight at short notice – arriving at bridge site at 9.30 hrs. 27 August. Leading platoon was in time to see the assault crossing of River Seine. Watched by interested civilians on both banks. The enemy did not attend this performance . . . 1000 hrs – Order to commence work received. Work continued without respite. No major problems arose. There was no enemy shelling or mortaring of the site, although he was less than two miles away. 0200 hrs – bridge complete and open to traffic. The bridge was used almost from the moment of completion and heavy traffic including an armoured division streamed over it continuously. This was particularly gratifying to the men . . . the effect was most noticeable, in that all ranks, already very tired, worked extremely hard on maintenance of approaches".
(War Diary: WO171/1538, 27 August, 1944)*

30 Corps got our bridging after all – but there was a devil of a row about it.

But it was certainly needed. The bridges at their crossing point (Vernon) were destroyed. The infantry was ferried across under withering fire, then the race was on to get the armour across to save them from a desperate German counter-attack. Some armour and anti-tank

74

guns were rafted across. "Probably never before had so many engineer units or so much river crossing equipment been concentrated on the front of a single division engaged in an assault crossing." (Maj-Gen R.P. Pakenham-Walsh, The History of the Corps of R.E. *Vol. IX, Institution of R.E., Chatham, 1958, p. 383)*

Major Gen Bullen-Smith GOC 51 (H) Div has personally sworn vengeance on the 19th SS Panzer Div for an atrocity they committed at Routot. A farmer refused these thugs the wheels to his farmcart which he had hidden, so, his farm was burned down, his five-year-old daughter was bayoneted, his wife raped before his eyes and he kidnapped and forced to go along with the 19th SS. GOC 51st Highland Division is a man of his word as the Germans already know and is understudy to our Lt General John Crocker 1 Corps Commander. This is a good reminder of what we are fighting for.

Monday 28 August
6 Airborne div with their continental elements have captured Honfleur and are now standing opposite Le Havre. I think that they are to be sent back to England for a rest and to reform. They've done excellent work and their airborne landing will go down in history as one of the finest military feats. We take our hats off to the 6 Airborne.

"Our task for the time being was finished and we were to be sent back to England there to be prepared for what we knew not. It is hard to describe what this day in August meant to us. This was the first day since our landing in Normandy on 6th June that we had not been fighting. The feeling of relief was great indeed. Rest was what the men needed and sleep their first thought." (Gale, Op. cit. p. 149)

49 and 51 are racing neck and neck for the Seine, and Jerry can't get across. These two magnificent divisions are literally trampling the Hun underfoot. It's slaughter for he just won't give in. The American patrols are already half way between Paris and the German frontier. I wonder what the armchair critics are saying now. Today Supreme Headquarters of the Allied Expeditionary Force dared to come across the Channel and General Dwight Eisenhower is now Supreme Commander. Monty has relinquished command of the Americans to Gen Omar Bradley and is now simply Commander in Chief 21 Army Group, which is 2

British Army and 1 Cdn Army (thus 21). The Americans have given him a big write up, for on D Day he said he would be in Paris in 90 days and he made it I believe in 75. He put the Yanks there too and not British troops.

Tuesday 29 August
49 and 51 are after Rouen so we prepare to move closer behind them. The Boche won't try to defend Rouen. He's got all on to just get across the Seine and scramble to safety. His ruined transport is holding up our advance and our POW camps are full up to the brim. I'll bet the Cdns' POW camps are empty though. We have counted so far in Cdn army alone 200,000 prisoners of war. They said they'd get to England and by jove they've made it.

Wednesday 30 August
We're across at Elbeuf and we're in Rouen. Corps HQ set up at Bois Ingers just south of the Seine. In my wildest dreams I never imagined such destruction could be inflicted on an army. The roads and fields and ditches are full of dead Germans, dead horses and smashed-up transport. What a stench there is in this hot weather. I look at these sights and register nothing. C'est la guerre, I suppose. I look and just don't seem to see. All I can think about is that the war is ending and quickly too. We get our instructions for our next role in the war. First Cdn Army have been given the honour of capturing Le Havre, Fécamp, St Valery and Dieppe then carrying on to Pas de Calais and clearing up the flying bomb sites. So it seems that we shall be left behind for a little while. 2 Cdn Corps are well over the Seine by now and their elements have reached Neufchatel. Their 2 Inf Div have specially asked to be allowed to take Dieppe for they want revenge on their comrades who fell there during the landing early on in the war.

Thursday 31 August
51st (H) Div are over the Seine now and are heading for St Valery where the Germans wiped out the original 51 in 1940.

From May to June, 1940, the 51st Highland Division had fought a rearguard action while the B.E.F. was being evacuated from Dunkirk. After twelve days of remorseless fighting with ammunition almost exhausted, the 51st was trapped in St Valery. British ships were prevented from reaching them by German artillery. On 12 June they had no alternative but to surrender to the forces of Rommel. Up to

1,000 were killed and 8,000 taken prisoner. Rennie's message to the 51st on 31 August, 1944, was : "We of the Highland Division must not rest till we have freed our kith and kin of the St Valery Highland Division and avenged their misfortune to the full". (Salmond, Op. cit. p. 171)

There are no more Germans left on this side of the Seine now; they have all been accounted for. It will take a bigger army of L of C (*Lines of Communication*) troops to clear up this mess than it took to inflict it on the Hun. This headlong gallop of our armies has been a terrible strain on the sappers. Bridging at speed is difficult, but never once have we failed the armies, never once have they been held up whilst waiting for a bridge. On top of this we have had mine clearance, road maintenance, water supply and demolitions. I'm just about dead beat, but so terribly enthusiastic and happy for the war will soon be over.

The log of the Chief Engineer's War Diary, 1st British Corps, is incredibly full at this time, dealing each day with a huge amount of work: dealing with unexploded bombs, booby traps and mines, building bridges (sometimes under fire), laying tracks, shifting supplies, water supply, testing the effects of mines, conducting recces and airfield construction. No wonder he was 'dead beat'.

The Americans have passed Rheims and are dashing for the German border, Brit 2 Army captured Beauvais and are en route to Amiens.

Friday 1 Sept
49 Div can't wait to get across the Seine by the bridges so they are ferrying and rafting their way across.

Cpl Graham Roe's Commanding Officer (Hallamshire Battalion) could not wait to make the 60 km. round trip to use the bridge at Rouen to cross the Seine, so 'C' Company crossed in rowing boats. At the other side, his 35 lb radio set and other equipment weighed him down in the thick mud and he had to be hauled out with great difficulty by hanging on to a rifle butt. Three peasants watched with interest. One pointed to Cpl Roe's machine gun and persisted "mitraillette, mitraillette", which in the confusion sounded like "me try it, me try it". Covered in mud and exhausted, Cpl Roe's response was not very accommodating.

Everything seems to be very blurred just now. Yanks are in Verdun; the Huns in Dieppe went yellow and wouldn't take 2 Cdn Div on for a second time so they beat it. Canucks have now Dieppe.

"this Division had assaulted the beaches in the great raid of 1942. It had seemed likely that the enemy would fight for this port, and we had accordingly made arrangements to deliver against it a shattering attack, in which very heavy bombardment by air and sea would be the prelude to the land assault. But Operation 'Fusilade' never took place. When the 8th Reconnaissance Regiment reached Dieppe on the morning of 1 September it found the enemy gone. The only obstacle to the passage of its armoured cars and carriers through the streets was, it recorded, 'the dense crowds of Dieppe citizens, who were shouting, crying, throwing flowers and generally climbing all over our vehicles in the mad joy of liberation'." The Division stood down for a few days and was able to honour the graves of the dead of 1942. (C.P. Stacey, The Canadian Army, 1939–1945, Ottawa, 1948, p. 211)

30 Corps will have Amiens soon. Nothing can stop this all victorious army. I bet everybody is excited at home. Hope the mail is getting there alright.

Saturday 2 Sept
51st Highland Div smothered St Valery last night and in the words of the CRE they slew the —— lot. Very few prisoners were taken. They showed a little fight but the Jocks were on form.

It was a time for avenging old defeats. When the 51st recaptured St Valery, its C.O. General Rennie, who had himself been captured there in 1940, but managed to escape, deployed his brigades in positions as close as possible to those which their predecessors had occupied in 1940. He chose as his H.Q. the château at Cailleville where General Fortune's H.Q. had been at the time of the surrender. A memorial service was held on 3 September for the dead of 1940.

49th West Riding Div were not going to be outdone either. They simply scampered across country and scared the living daylights out of the Huns in Fécamp. I hope the Yorkshiremen don't drink all the Benedictine there.

16. The Basilica at La Deliverande.

17. Royal Engineers crossing the
    River Orne at Thury Harcourt,
    south of Caen.

18. Blown German bridges, Moerdyk,
    Holland, November, 1944.

19. A knocked-out German Tiger Mark II tank, September, 1944.

20. Jan Pijnenburg, World Champion cyclist.

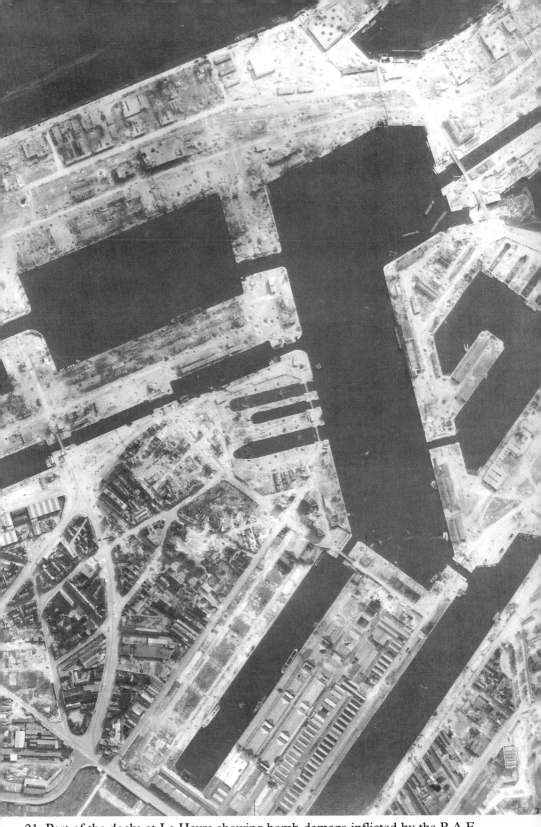

21. Part of the docks at Le Havre showing bomb damage inflicted by the R.A.F. when attacking the U-boat pens.

22. Tilburg, 1944.

23. The Château d'Audrieu, SS Headquarters, June, 1944.

24. Monique Livry-Level, witness to the Audrieu murders.

25. The grave of Major F.E.Hodge, CO of 'A' Company, Royal Winnipeg Rifles, a victim of the Audrieu murders. Beny-sur-Mer Military Cemetery.

26. The killings took place near this spot on 8 June, 1944.

PART OF RUINED FACTORY EAST OF CAEN SHOWING ABANDONED GERMAN SIDE-CAR FACTORY

BOMBED INERROF BY AMERICANS SHORTLY AFTER THIS DRAWING WAS MADE   (By kind permission of S.D.Robinson)

S D Robinson
7-8-44

28. This photograph is thought to show the bombing of Colombelles by the USAAF on 8 August, 1944.

29. Canadian vehicles on fire after the tragic bombing of Colombelles by the USAAF. *(K.Bell, National Archives of Canada, PA 115862)*

30. The German garrison being rounded up in Middelburg by men of the 7th/9th Royal Scots, November, 1944.

31. The iron and steel works at Colombelles after the bombing.

They certainly had a good try. Cpl Roe of the 49th division had his first brush with Benedictine. "The Col. detailed four of us to take a jeep and go to the Benedictine monastery at Fécamp, north of Le Havre and buy as many bottles as we could carry in a jeep! It must be said that we had no idea where the enemy was, and many miles to cover with only a vague idea where the Monastery was located. So it was with trepidation and foreboding, that we set off into this journey into the unknown, armed to the teeth and without a map, hoping that the enemy had fled or withdrawn into Le Havre! We kept close to the banks of the River Seine for most of the way and struck north from the estuary as it widened. It was dark when we arrived at Fécamp after much searching and probing. We banged on the huge door of the Monastery, which was eventually opened by a monk who must have travelled from the bowels of the earth judging by the time it took him. The Lieut. who was in charge of our party had difficulty in getting it across to him that we had come to buy Benedictine, and I was able to help him out with my contribution of schoolboy French, but he would let us have only one large bottle each, accompanied by two miniatures. No matter how we pleaded, that was it. We now had to make our way back to our last known location through what we regarded as 'no man's land' and try to find our comrades. No easy task this, because it was not uncommon for units to be moved at a moment's notice and there were no signposts to give us directions, because no one from the British Army had reached this far yet, only us. After many hours, as dawn was just breaking we found our comrades and reported to the Col. The Lieut. got a reprimand from him because he did not believe that we had been allowed only one large bottle per person, and wanted to know what we had done with the rest. We did not tell him that we had drunk the miniatures on the way back as some kind of recompense and reward for the hazardous journey we had endured on his behalf. This was my very first taste of Benedictine. It was most pleasant, though rather syrupy."

The Americans are but 11 miles from GERMANY PROPER. I reckon I'll lose the sweep. Our work is terrific. I must make a mighty mental effort to prevent myself from 'flagging' on this last lap to victory; I am terribly tired and can't remember when I last slept. We are all working like fanatics. There is no longer any distinction between officers and men, we just work furiously side by side. Next job is Le Havre. I wonder if the squareheads will decide to hang on here a little; they've got good defence works. Perhaps they won't surrender. If they don't then we'll put the RAF and a couple of Victory shoots on them. That will persuade them to come out.

Sunday 3 Sept

Now that our Divs are across the Seine we must dash after them, so today we pushed our way through all the debris of a broken army, up to Elbeuf and crossed the Seine on a 400ft floating Bailey bridge which had been constructed by 2 Cdn Corps Engineers. Elbeuf is the dirtiest, filthiest and smelliest place I have ever seen in or out of the war. For sheer squalor this place beats the band, dirty narrow streets full of dirty people, all stunted and ugly, waving like mad and screaming 'cigarette pour papa'. If the jeep stopped we were instantly besieged and smothered with females. They were genuinely overjoyed to see us. We gave them cigarettes and food. The Seine was a ghastly sight where we crossed – swollen bodies of horses were floating about and there were many dead Nazis lying on the banks. The stench was revolting and made me 'rift'. After Elbeuf we went on to Rouen. Movement was difficult. The same old story of smashed German transport and guns, horses and men and lines of haggard prisoners waiting for transport to our PW cages. Rouen is a fine old city and I was surprised at the small amount of damage there. The people gave us a rousing welcome and bedecked the jeep with garlands of flowers and at one time it was impossible to find a way through the excited crowd. We were hugged and kissed and cheered right through the place. It was good to see these people looking so happy. After 80 miles we stopped at a little village called Foucard. We were the first allied troops they had seen and they gave us everything they had.

Monday 4 Sept

I slept 12 solid hours after doing 39 non-stop and so today I feel very fit and well. I had a lovely wash and clean up in a farmyard and felt great after it. The sun has turned me almost black but the recent heavy going seems to have given me a tired look. However we will get a breather before the Le Havre job, for planning does not start for a few days yet. It is rumoured that the Guards Armoured Division with Second Army have liberated Brussels. If this is so they must have done the fastest advance of the war.* I sincerely hope that we don't have to go up through Belgium and

* They had entered Brussels on 3 September.

80

Holland. I can't see the necessity. If we carry on to Germany then the Hun will have to evacuate Holland to protect his own country. It will take a long time to clear those two as well.

Tuesday 5 Sept
Today we crept a little nearer Le Havre to a tiny village called Mannville le Goupil passing through Bolbec en route. Bolbec seems quite a nice little town and if possible I must try and get back there for a look round. It seems a little strange now that we have broken out of that awful bridgehead. We feel as though we can stretch a little. 2 Cdn Corps are carrying on clearing up the Pas de Calais and the flying bomb sites. I thought we would have had this job, but it seems to me that there is going to be a bit of a 'do' at Le Havre first. The operation is to be called Astonia and 49 West Riding Div are playing the major role with 51st Highland Div acting as a stop block to the north of the port. The defences must be pretty tough for we are also having the assistance of 42 Assault Regt Royal Engineers and the 34 Tank Bde and 33 Armd Bde.* Our intelligence tells us that there are some 7000 – 8000 Germans in Le Havre and something like 40,000 civilians.† The Germans' morale is supposed to be a little low but they have had instructions from their Führer that they must hang on to the last man and the last gun. They have some excellent defence works – a replica of those at Brest which have kept the Yanks at bay for 36 days. We will see.

Wednesday 6 Sept
Astonia planning is now finished and our divs are in position. The CE has 'tee-d' up 42 Aslt Regt's work and we are very interested for this is their first action. We are wasting no time on this job. 1000 Lancasters were put on tonight and I stood and watched them rain down their 12,000 bombs. I felt a little sorry for the civilians in there. Jerry won't let them come out – he says they know too much.

*In the 4 years that they had held the city, the Germans had built every kind of barrier – concrete dug-outs and concrete gun emplacements, minefields, an anti-tank ditch on every possible approach. The defensive line was one mile deep in parts. There were also the natural barriers of the Seine in the south and the sea to the north-west. The actual port defences however, were weak and incomplete.
† The garrison was 12,000 strong, but many troops were unfit and elderly, so effective strength was 8,000.

As Cpl Graham Roe and his comrades of the Hallamshire Battalion waited outside Le Havre while the pattern bombing took place, they were covered with ash and charred fragments of school exercise books which had wafted back from the town. One tank commander who refused to take part in the attack and bombardment of Le Havre, arguing that civilian lives would be lost unnecessarily, was William Douglas-Home (brother of a future Prime Minister). He was stripped of his captain's rank, cashiered and sentenced to one year's hard labour for disobeying orders. Three thousand civilians died as a result of the bombing of Le Havre, though there were few enemy casualties from the bombardment. Again, as at Caen, rumour must have been rife about the status of the civilians. The Commandant of Fortress Le Havre, Col. Eberhard Wildermuth, had under his care about 60,000 French civilians when he took over command. He was concerned about their evacuation and on 21 August issued a proclamation resulting in about 10,000 leaving the town. But most civilians wanted to stay on, supported by the Resistance Movement. Wildermuth therefore had to use force to clear the town, but this was halted with the onset of the siege.

I think our chaps will have a go either late tonight or early in the morning. This is the first big attack of this campaign ever to be carried out in the dark.

Thursday 7 Sept
What atrocious luck. At 22.00 hrs there was a cloudburst and the operation has had to be postponed. Our tanks are bogged down and sappers will have to make Corduroy roads right to the very gates of the city. These roads are constructed of logs split down the middle and although they take a long time to lay they are excellent for tanks. We used to be often visited by Capt Stewart's brother, a Canadian in the Glengarry Highlanders. He was a very cheery chap. We have just heard he was killed yesterday with 2 Cdn Corps in the Pas de Calais. This is the first time we have had peaceful nights and raid free since D Day. All we hear now is just the artillery's continual bombardment on the Le Havre defences. The KOYLIs are the nearest just now, but they daren't make a move without tank support. Liège is liberated.

Friday 8 Sept

If everything goes according to what Dr Horton has foreseen then today should be Mary's D Day and I will be a father. This thought is distracting my mind from the war effort. I'll be uneasy now until I hear the news from home. Our mail is coming through very badly just now. Rain is still stopping play at Le Havre. I wish they would get cracking. Just to stoke things up a little the Lancs dropped another 1500 tons on them. I can't see that the port is going to be much use to us anyway, for the RAF have been pounding this place ever since the war began, and now Jerry is to be heard doing extensive demolitions to the port and harbour installations. More heavy rain this evening. But now I sleep in a tent and no longer in a trench. A ground sheet is not altogether proof against this torrential rain – but a good rum issue is – and I sleep like a top.

Saturday 9 Sept

The attack has been postponed again.* The waiting must be driving the chaps crazy. Everywhere is a quagmire and the sappers are working like mad making roads right up to the enemy guns, in the dark. At 1200 hrs each day since the siege began the ADC of 49 Div visits the German commander in Le Havre and over a glass of wine they talk terms of surrender, but Hitler has spoken by radio direct to this squarehead and he's scared stiff of his Führer. Furthermore he says we won't get through his defences, but he's never heard of the Assault Engineers. Neither has anybody else for that matter, for they are still on the 'secret' list.

Sunday 10 Sept

This morning the weather was brilliant and looked as though it had every intention of remaining so. Everybody is keyed up and awaiting 42nd's opening attack this evening. Brig Campbell and the Corps Commander with the BGS are on the scene. We get a bird's eye view from way back. At 1900 hrs the Assault sappers went in on their first job and they performed like veterans, although we could make nothing out clearly. There was a terrific

---

* This did not stop an official Wehrmacht report announcing in Berlin on 9 September that the grand attack had begun, describing the gallantry of the defenders and giving figures for the number of Allied guns knocked out.

artillery barrage put up and Jerry replied with all he had. Huge columns of smoke were rising from the city. In 40 minutes after the attack we got the news that the sappers had wiped out 11 strongpoints and the Germans were mystified by these armoured engineers with their 5 secret weapons.

It might be appropriate to consider at this point, the work of the assault engineers at Le Havre as an example of their sterling efforts throughout the North-West Europe campaign. This was a night attack, so they operated by 'Monty's moonlight' – searchlights reflected off the clouds. Their armoury included Churchill AVREs, Sherman Flails (or Crabs), Crocodiles, Churchill bridgelayers, armoured bulldozers, sledges, fascines and snakes. The latter consisted of a fireman's hose installed in a carrier and towed behind a Churchill. A rocket took the hose 250 yards across the ground, when it was blown by liquid explosive (nitro-glycerine) which in turn would blow mines by sympathetic detonation. Their tasks involved creating lanes through minefields, breaking roadblocks, bridging rivers and crossing ditches, creating gaps in the defences and making routes as well as clearing the enemy.

Forming up for D Day was difficult because of 48 hours of non-stop rain. "Unfortunately, many of the flails got bogged climbing out of the Lazarde Valley and they were arriving in the F.A.A. in driblets up to 1630 hrs on D Day. This left a bare minimum of time for the final tying up, netting and forming up of the gapping teams. However, the gapping teams just managed to marry up in time although the wedding ceremony was somewhat curtailed by the late arrival of the bridegroom." (War Diary 42nd Assault Regiment R.E.: WO 171/1805, 10 September, 1944) The War Diary details countless snags and much resourcefulness was called upon. The flails missed some deep mines, and mines in standing corn or muddy ground. On the use of the snake, the War Diary reports: "The lane commander (Lane 1) now recconoitred a place where he could just cross the ditch at as sharp an angle as he dared and swung his team at it. His snake was pushed successfully over and was being adjusted when an enormous explosion knocked everyone flat. It was the snake in Lane 2 going off. Snake 1 was now blown, knocking everyone in Lane 2 flat". The assault bridge carried by 617 Assault Squadron must have caused a great deal of consternation. "This bridge travelled for 6000 yards at about ½ m.p.h. throughout the night, led by a L/Cpl on a motor-bike. It moved through the lanes, through Area 'A', down the hill, through the wood into the valley, and finally fell off within 100 yards of its destination – so near and yet so far. Its downfall was due to the fact that the AVRE went over two bumps in rapid succession, and the bridge jumped off . . ."

Nevertheless, their achievements were considerable and the troops showed immense fortitude against great problems. There were many examples of initiative, for example, when two AVREs of 222 Assault Squadron approaching from Harfleur "encountered a previously unknown anti-tank ditch. As they had no fascine bundles with them, they had to blow down trees to fill up the ditch. This was done under shell, mortar and machine-gun fire". The opening of this route enabled the Hallamshire Battalion to advance. These same two AVREs then went on to destroy a roadblock with a flying dustbin, and then to tackle a small German barracks taking 300 prisoners whom they held until infantry arrived. The Royal Engineers' history says of this episode: "The whole operation was one of the most extensive examples of the cooperation of assault engineers with other arms and field companies in a 'set piece' attack undertaken in the course of the war. It demonstrates clearly the value of armoured engineers in carrying out work under such fire that field units could not have hoped to survive". (Pakenham-Walsh, Op. cit., p. 388)

Monday 11 Sept.
The attack proper began at 22.30 hrs and the sappers were withdrawn from the fray after a brilliant performance, with exceedingly small casualties too. The Corps Commander granted quite a few immediate awards to these chaps. This morning KOYLIs of the 49 Div had forced their way right into the town and at noon were in bitter street fighting. 51 Div who were playing stopping block to the north of the city couldn't resist having a go.*At noon also they sent in a report that the Black Watch had practically got through to the harbour! These are two fine divs and I'm sure the whole German army could never stop them. There is much bitterness in 1 Corps as the 9 p. m. news said that the Cdns had entered Le Havre. There are no Cdns near here for miles – they are all in Belgium just now. This is the result of us being in the Cdn Army. There are as many Englishmen in the Cdn Army as there are Cdns.†

* Major A.N. Parker of the Camerons reached a strongpoint in the outer defences and used a captured German telephone to get through to the Garrison Commander offering him the choice to surrender or be annihilated. He did not receive a satisfactory reply, so the Camerons carried on.
† 1st British Corps had been part of the First Canadian Army since 22 July.

Tuesday 12 Sept

Le Havre fell at 11 am. I'm afraid our intelligence people were a little off their mark when they said there were but 7000 – 8000 Germans in the place. We've taken 11,000 prisoners by teatime today.* The Garrison Commander aged 29 was very arrogant at the surrender and when GOC 49 Div offered to shake his hand, Garrison Commander spat in his face. The Commander was severely wounded during the fray and I suppose this prevented him from getting his ears boxed for GOC 49 Div is a tough customer.

If the story was true, it might have something to do with the fact that the Garrison Commander's wife and children had been killed in a Berlin raid. Col. Wildermuth who was severely wounded by a shell splinter in the left thigh, had to surrender at about 12 noon from his concrete dug-out in the gardens of Fort Tourville. His last words before surrender were a gracious compliment to his opponents: "The correct and gentlemanly behaviour of British officers and men towards the wounded and prisoners filled every German officer and man with respect". (Special Interrogation Report of Col. E. Wildermuth, Staff College, Camberley: WO 223/72, p. 8) Maj-Gen E. Barker, G.O.C. 49th Division was as my father described him. On taking command of the Division, he had altered the divisional flash by insisting that the polar bear's head be raised in a proud, defiant stance.

Full honours for this battle went to the Hallamshires, but don't tell 51st (H) Div.

The achievements of the Hallamshire Battalion were remarkable. Cpl Roe remembers: "The Hallamshires' advance was along a road leading to a steel rolling mill about half-way along on a down gradient with the high ground on our right. No sooner had we reached the rolling mill when murderous fire poured on us from our right where we could now observe many concrete emplacements all the way along the hillside, previously camouflaged. I made a dive for cover among the discarded rolls which are cylindrical steel metal rolls, used for rolling iron billets into thick wire ready for finer drawing down. Easy for me to recognize as such. They were virtually the same as those used at the

---

* Many of the surrendering German carried printed bills, dropped by Allied aircraft, saying how kind the Allies were to their prisoners, and finishing up with: "This man is to be well treated and sent back from the front as soon as possible. Signed Eisenhower and Montgomery."

*firm I worked for before I was called up. Most of my comrades
followed me into the scrap yard otherwise we would have been sitting
targets. The only danger was that we could still be hit by ricochets from
the numerous heavy metal rolls. A variety of weapons was trained on
us but the most effective from the enemy's point of view, were the rapid
firing and deadly accurate 20 mm cannons. I could see that some of my
comrades were unable to find enough protection with the inevitable
consequences. The chatter of multiple machine-gun fire continued
mercilessly, causing a fireworks type of display among the iron rolls as
they ricocheted many times about them. It seemed that there was no
escape. I prayed. Always under conditions of intense shelling,
bombing, machine-gun and small arms fire, I could taste 'hot metal'.
This has since been explained to me as the ammonia in the human
constitution reacting with the iron in one's bloodstream and mani-
festing itself in the taste buds brought on by fear. And under this
present situation the 'hot metal' taste was very strong indeed. There
was nothing we could do until we could call up some aid which I did
on my 18 set because I did not know where the Major had taken refuge.
The C.O. must have heard my call or knew of our dilemma. A
squadron of Churchill tanks appeared at the top of the rise from which
we had started our advance, and began 'posting' H.E. shells into the
slits of the pillboxes set in the hillside, silencing each one in turn. Their
accuracy was uncanny. They saved some of our lives, of that there was
no doubt. I gave thanks and counted my blessings once again."*

*When they eventually reached the docks, the War Diary modestly
claims that the four companies cleared the dock area just before
midnight, capturing 1,005 prisoners, a submarine, three Dornier
Flying Boats, and clearing an area 7,000 yards from east to west, and
200 yards in width, including dozens of pillboxes.*

There were 5000 civilians killed in the battle, 350 of them were
suffocated in a huge air-raid shelter. Even so, the others gave our
troops a right royal welcome. The docks are 'kaput' and a large
portion of the town is also badly damaged. Food and water and
medical supplies are being rushed in today. The total length of the
actual fighting was 36 hours from start to finish. 49 Div reported
approx 400 casualties, 250 of these wounded – remarkable. 51
have not yet reported but they will be lighter still.* The Germans
had a good life in Le Havre and lived off the fat of the land. They
were mostly naval personnel.

* Their casualties were thirteen officers and 120 other ranks.

Wednesday 13 Sept
Went into Le Havre with Capt Stewart this morning. We couldn't get right into the city but had to stay on the outskirts. The damage didn't seem too bad to me, not after Caen, Falaise and Lisieux. The prisoners were streaming out and they looked about the best lot I have so far seen, but this was their first action in this campaign too. I saw infantrymen of 49 and 51 drinking Benedictine and Cherry Brandy – two very fine liqueurs – out of the bottle and then bashing it up against the wall. They were very drunk indeed. This is only to be expected after such a victory. It is the reaction from that awful pent up feeling one gets after waiting three or four days for the attack to begin. I felt like joining in with them.† Today the Americans got over the German border – well done the Yanks. This is great news. I still think the war will be over by 15 Oct – Jerry has nothing left at all. To reorganise his armies just now would take a bigger effort than even he is capable of, and in my opinion organisation in the German army is the finest of any army in the world.

Thursday 14 Sept
Another quick dash down to Le Havre with Capt Knight and this time I get the Garrison Commander's sheets for a souvenir and a box of his cigars for father. Our Corps Troops RE are sleeping in the most lavish hotels. It looked very funny to see the sanitary man sleeping in the Bridal Suite – these French hotels are really lavish too. Corps Troops have the job of clearing up the debris and already have the bulldozers at work. We are now quiet for the first time since D Day. There is no work to do as both our Divs are resting. The nearest Germans are at Boulogne 200 miles away. British Second Army are up in Belgium; we are left all alone miles away from the fighting. I wonder what our new assignment will be – Belgium? Holland? or Germany? We will have to wait and see.

---

† Large quantities of food and drink were captured. "For the first time in the memory of those present, the Jocks had champagne in their tin mugs when they ate their evening meal. The news of the loot spread like wild-fire and we had to establish firm control to keep out hordes of the most desperate looters we have ever seen," wrote the C.O. of the 5/7th Gordons. The Brigade Major remarked: "It was harder to get into the fort after the 5/7th had captured it than when the Germans held it." (J.B. Salmond, Op. cit. p. 178)

Friday 15 Sept
All Belgium is now liberated. What a surprise and the biggest surprise is caused by the biggest mistake the Germans have made in the whole of this war, the fatheads. They defend broken-down ports like Le Havre, Brest, St Nazaire, Boulogne, Dunkerque etc. and when the leading elements of 7 Armd Div approached Antwerp they fled as fast as their horses and carts could carry them, leaving the port undamaged. Jerry, I'm surprised. This will definitely cost him the war. Antwerp is the second largest port in Europe, Hamburg being the largest, and of all the ports we would like the best, it is Antwerp. Well, we are mighty appreciative – won't be long now. Mary didn't make the grade on the 8th – instead she went to Doncaster! What a girl and me in a cold sweat.

Saturday 16 Sept
We are still resting but rumour has it that we will be pushing on to Belgium to take part of the front from Second Army, to the East of Antwerp. I don't like this. The French say that Belgium is the dirtiest of places and that the Belgians are not at all nice. This evening I had a walk down to the village and found an estaminet. I was with a Welsh friend. We sat and drank the vilest red wine at a most atrocious price too. The countryside is very dismal and now that I have not much work to do my thoughts turn to home and Mary. I keep wondering if the baby is born yet, and hope and pray that all will be well.

Sunday 17 Sept
Quite startling news today when we heard that the Allies had landed a large Airborne army in Northern Holland. News is scarce but this appears to be a brilliant move and looks like opening the gates for our armies to Germany. I didn't even know we had such an army. Shouldn't think they will meet much resistance.

Monday 18 Sept
The rains have returned and our two divs and Corps HQ begin their long trek to the battlefront once more.* The first leg of the journey takes us 75 miles to a village between Dieppe and Neufchatel called Smermesnil. This is about the most uncivilised

* This was a long trek with armour. The front was 200 miles away and had to be covered in three days.

and crude place I have ever seen. The people live like animals in their hovels. It's about time France had a good clean up. The people in this village don't even wear sabots and they are terribly dirty. I felt very sorry for the children. The villagers showed no sign of excitement when we arrived and seemed to have little interest in the war either.

Tuesday 19 Sept
I visited a flying bomb site this morning. It was hidden away in a wood and was excellently camouflaged. The RAF had been at it as was evident by the 40' craters in all the fields around the place. The main part consisted of a huge concrete runway or launching platform, about 100 yds in length and sloping from 0 ft to about 30 ft. This platform pointed directly at London. The buildings nearby were built very strongly and the whole wood was defended by shelters of the Tobruk type and by machine gun emplacements too. The artillery had been used to finally 'kill' the place as 2 Cdn Corps had swept through. Remnants of flying bombs were to be found, but these had all been destroyed by the Germans. At long last Brest has fallen.

Wednesday 20 Sept
We seem to be taking our time on this trip to Belgium and today was spent cooking and eating eggs which we got from the villagers for chocolate and cigarettes. The Airborne army have captured an important bridge at Arnhem. There is not another crossing of the Rhine for 50 miles each way. I think Jerry has 'had' this war and should pack up any minute. The general opinion here is that Jerry will NOT fight on his own soil. I don't think he will. Mr Churchill has just said that the war will end a lot sooner than we dared once to expect, and Churchill is usually very guarded in his speeches.

Thursday 21 Sept
Off again in a huge convoy and first halt is 100 miles from Smermesnil in a wood near Cambrai. We are the first troops in this district other than the Cdns and the Northern French like the English very much. Perhaps they remember our fathers here before us. We passed the graves of the last war. They were in a very good condition, well kept, neat and tidy. A runaway German Tiger tank had crashed through the wall of one of these cemeteries and had burned out about 2 yards from the grave of a dead Tommy. These graveyards are very big places and there are

hundreds of graves in each one. The French gave us fruit and wine and cheered us all along the route. Today our little mascot, a fox terrier puppy which we rescued from Caen and called Cress (Corps RE Signal Section) was playing in the road when the convoy halted – along came a jeep at terrific speed – Cress was buried with full military honours on the roadside between Cambrai and Valenciennes near a last war graveyard.*

Friday 22 Sept
On the move again today in pouring rain we pass through Valenciennes – Mons – Waterloo – Brussels arriving late at night at a pretty little Belgian village called Keerbergen. It was quite a thrill to pass through Waterloo and I am sure father would have liked to have been there too. The lion on top of the hill is a land-mark for miles. Brussels is a beautiful city and I saw little or no damage, the buildings were grand and the shops seem to have plenty of wares for sale. The people appeared nicely dressed and were still excited by the sight of British troops. They gave us a 'big hand'. I have never eaten so much fruit before, grapes, apples, peaches and pears. The Cdns captured Boulogne this evening.

Saturday 23 Sept
What a surprise! We are now occupying some brand new Belgian barracks and we are made very comfortable indeed. Sleeping on the floor is far better than sleeping on the ground and this has been our lot since D Day. We have outstripped our two Divs and will have to wait a few days until they take up their places once more in the line. 1 Pol Armoured Division came under command 1 Corps today. Planning on future ops is to begin tomorrow. Our Brigadiers had a conference with the Corps Commander today. Jerry has to be kept on the run, for given the slightest chance he will reorganise.

---

* The irony of passing through former battlegrounds was not lost on others who made that same dash in late September. The *Yorkshire Pud* describes the journey of the Duke of Wellington's Regiment: "On September 21st we moved in one bound through Abbeville and Arras to Tournai...Here and there we passed the cemeteries (still beautifully kept) of our predecessors who fought the same implacable, fierce and baleful enemy...Mont St Eloi and Vimy Ridge looked down on us, this new Army sweeping through on wheels and tracks where in 1916, '17 and '18 an advance of 100 yards could only be gained at a tremendous price in British and Canadian lives." (Op. cit., pp. 12–13)

Sunday 24 Sept

We all had a holiday today whilst our divs get in position I suppose. Out came all the second battledresses and, although caked with Normandy mud, a good stiff brush soon removed it. The batmen provided an iron and we managed to press the trousers. Boots were polished for the first time this side of the Channel and by afternoon we were looking quite smart. We all had an invitation to visit Keerbergen and join in the liberation celebrations this evening. What a relief to have an evening out, and what celebrations. Every cafe and every house was chock full of soldiers and civilians. Everybody was laughing and dancing and singing. It was good to hear these people sounding so happy. I think this must be the first time they laughed since the Germans came in '40. We were the guests of honour and were treated as such. They gave us all they'd got. We even had ice cream of a sort and beer – very weak. The French told us that the Belgians weren't so good and that they were dirty. I think the boot is on the other foot. These people are good, clean living, generous and honest. Their houses are the finest I have ever seen I think. Our two draughtsmen say that even we have nothing on them for architecture and I can quite believe it too, unless Keerbergen is an exception.

Monday 25 Sept

Although I think Belgium is a very nice place and the people in it are nice too, I feel a little depressed because ever since I came here, I never thought we would have to clear up these countries. Looks to me as though we'll have to go to Holland too. I thought we would have made straight for Germany proper, but I suppose the War Lords know best. Anyway Jerry hasn't stopped running yet, but he's going to get some good defence lines along these canals. Our sappers are working like madmen to construct bridges quickly enough to keep our army close on Jerry's heels. We need a very great amount of bridging for all the bridges have been blown either by the RAF or by the retreating Germans. Things aren't going so good with the Airborne boys up at Arnhem. Today we saw two lots of reinforcements going up to them. They have been subsisting on one-sixth of their normal rations.

Tuesday 26 Sept

I am amazed at our quiet nights we are having these days; we hear little or no explosions and our sleep in quite uninterrupted. Brig

Campbell has been in trouble again. He went up to the Albert canal to inspect a bridge being built by 49 Div. Jerry opened up with his mortars and got a direct hit, killed 4 sappers and wounded the Brig in the head and arm. He refuses to go either to hospital or be evacuated to England but the old warhorse will go when the ambulance comes.

Wednesday 27 Sept
Our divs in position and we push on again to a little village which was freed only two days ago and is about a mile behind the front line. Sandoven is its name and after Keerbergen it looks very dull. The villagers peep at us through their windows as we pass through and there are still the signs of battle about the place. Once more we are under canvas. The ground is saturated by the recent heavy rainfalls, but I have managed to scrounge a German officer's small iron hospital type bed. I'm *not* having any more trenches. I'll sleep on the 'deck'. Might as well be killed by a bomb or a shell as die of pneumonia. Heavy artillery in the nearby fields provides our bedtime lullaby once more and the acrid smell of cordite fills our nostrils again.

Thursday 28 Sept
Well 49 are the first to get the ball rolling on the 1 Corps front. The sappers got three class 70 bridges up today over the important Escaut canal and the infantry captured Herenthals. The Poles with elements of 2 Cdn Corps are pushing out north of Antwerp but are having to fight for every foot of ground. Jerry I'm afraid has got a little organised in that district and even though he is slowly withdrawing he is putting up good resistance. Calais is still holding out to the Cdns and the commander has refused the ultimatum. Under cover of evacuating refugees from the city he has heavily mined all main roads leading in. This is a typical Nazi trick, but he's 'had' Calais for 4 AGRA have got their guns trained on the place.

Friday 29 Sept
I've been feeling anything but happy recently, for either yesterday or today was Mary's D Day. I've really got the wind up and every DR (*Dispatch Rider*) that comes I think he has a telegram for me. I hope and pray that all is well. If only I could be there with her. Instead of which I am in the most miserable environment, locked in a life and death struggle with a defeated nation of fanatics, in

pouring rain – and on top of this I have a terrible cold. Second British Army are fighting like madmen to get to our airborne chaps at Nijmegen, for they are getting the worst of this deal and have already lost Arnhem but still hold the Nijmegen bridge. I hope Gen Dempsey makes the grade. Our casualties are very heavy so far. We have lost 3 men in every 5. I had a trip into Lierre this afternoon. This is the first Belgian town I have had a look at. We went to the mobile bath unit. It is about the size of Doncaster, rather cold and dismal and the shops, quite empty, are only very small for a town of this size. I was warmed up a little with a glass of Pernod which a civilian kindly bought me. Cigarettes in Lierre will fetch 1 franc each, therefore 100 fags can be sold for 11/3d. Black Market is rife in this town.

Saturday 30 Sept
Today came the news that I have been awaiting. Mary gave birth to a son on the 27th and, although she had a tough time of it, both mother and son are doing fine – what a relief. I feel like going out and licking Jerry on my own. Recently I became so miserable about everything in general that I felt like going out to Jerry and chucking in the sponge. I feel a new man, even my cold has disappeared. If only we had a bottle, we could celebrate. That, however is impossible, so we decided it must be at the first opportunity.*
Last night three German Olympic swimming champions propelled a mine 8 miles down the river to the Nijmegen bridge and succeeded in causing quite an amount of damage to one of the pillars. This was a very fine feat and the swimmers were picked up exhausted on their return journey. The bridge however is repairable and the sappers have got the work well in hand already and I believe are preparing to construct two more Baileys alongside.

A huge reinforced concrete bridge over a 300-yard wide river, this was one of the most important Allied held bridges in Western Europe. The Germans could not afford to let the Allies make use of it. On 28 September eighty-one prisoners were captured, many of them hidden as snipers in the girders. Royal Engineers troops disconnected explo-

* L. Cpl Roy Cullingworth R.E., who was with my father at the time, told me that my father had had sympathy pains at the time of the birth, even though he was separated by the war from my mother. I had never heard this story before, but, knowing of his devotion, it sounds right!

sive charges under sniper fire and made the bridge safe. Also on that same day, the Germans tried to bomb the bridge. On the 29th the swimmers guided mines, linked in pairs by cables, around the piers. One pier in the railway bridge was demolished and a hole blown in the roadway of the road bridge. But the road bridge was quickly repaired by the insertion of two Bailey spans.

Chapter Eight

The Freeing of the Scheldt

The next obvious strategic target was the crossing of the Rhine. Before any attempt could be made, however, elaborate preparations and a vast build-up of forces and supplies had to be made. The supply problem became crucial. For instance, the Allied armies were consuming a million gallons of petrol a day, fuel which was still being transported over stretched lines of communication from the Normandy ports. Antwerp had been captured on 4 September. Its docks, less than 100 miles from the front line, could unload twenty times as much as Dieppe, which was 300 miles from the fighting. But these facilities could not be used by the Allies while the Scheldt estuary remained in German hands.

Operations to clear the estuary began from Antwerp on 2 October. Operation Switchback from 6 October involved the 3rd Canadian Infantry Division clearing the flooded land from the Leopold Canal to the south bank of the Scheldt, to provide a launching area for subsequent seaborne landings on Walcheren and Beveland. Here they met fierce German resistance and difficult ground conditions. The last pockets of resistance in the Breskens area were not cleared until 3 November. The Canadians paid dearly. A second attack by the 2nd Canadian Infantry Division came in from the east across the Beveland Isthmus in late October, supported by the 52nd Lowland Division, which landed on the southern part of Beveland (Operation Vitality I and II). By 4 November the Lowland Division had pushed across the Causeway which connected Beveland with Walcheren and the Engineers managed to effect a crossing over the treacherous, muddy channel which separated the two. An occupied area 2,000 yards deep and two miles wide was established on Walcheren.

Walcheren, the island at the mouth of the estuary and the last German stronghold, was taken as a result of an amphibious operation from 1 to 8 November. The operation was in two parts. Operation

Infatuate I and II involved the 52 (Lowland) Division assault on Flushing, and the 4th Special Service Brigade landings at Westkapelle respectively. The campaign was severely hindered by the flooding of certain areas, first by the R.A.F. to hamper German supplies and movement, and then by the Germans themselves.

The port of Antwerp was opened twenty days later when the seventy-mile channel which connected it with the sea was cleared of mines. The long period from the original capture of the port to its final opening 85 days later was a supply nightmare for the Allies and gave Hitler time that he was soon to put to good effect.

Meanwhile, the British Second Army and 1st British Corps pushed on through Holland towards the Maas, capturing Tilburg in late October, while the U.S. First Army took the offensive against the Siegfried Line leading to the capture of Aachen, and the Third Army battled it out in Luxembourg and Lorraine.

Sunday 1 Oct

Although the British Second Army have now pushed over the German frontier and the Americans are also slowly forcing a way to Aachen, I'm beginning to think that I have lost the sweep, perhaps not by a lot though, for it is only this country that is slowing down our advance. Jerry though, I believe, is getting a little more organised. He's a marvel at organisation. 21 Army Group have now set up shop in Brussels. They would be sure to pick the best of places. It becomes so cold at night in these fields that it is difficult to work and I have heard that the BGS is looking out for billets indoors.

Monday 2 Oct

All our divs are busy bridging the numerous canals, Jerry has evacuated Turnhout, the Poles are pushing north of Antwerp and the Huns are bewailing their loss of this magnificent port. They realise now what a terrible mistake they made and are bombing and shelling the place in the hope of putting the docks out of action. I think it is too late now. Our artillery have departed this location and all is quiet once more. I suppose we are due for a move any day now.

Tuesday 3 Oct

There is quite a battle developing just north of Antwerp but the Poles are getting the best of it. Jerry attacked the port with one-man submarines, flying bombs and a new weapon, the V2, about which I know very little yet. 2 Army are fanning out around Nijmegen and most of the Airborne boys – the remains I should say – are being evacuated to England.

Wednesday 4 Oct
The American First Army under 'Blood and Guts' Patton are now four miles through the Siegfried Line. The going is very tough and our intelligence tells us that at this place the Line is at its weakest. The Americans have no assault engineers, but their infantry are trained a little on similar lines and use a weapon called the Reddy Fox, but this has not the power of the Beehive (*explosive charges*) and so the defences are proving a hard nut to crack. One especially strong pillbox was overcome by a bulldozer getting to the rear and completely burying the place.

Thursday 5 Oct
The weather has forced us to take more substantial shelter and so today we moved into 'The Caserne' in Turnhout. These are really splendid barracks and our predecessors were the SS. They have kept the place spick and span considering that they had to leave in a hurry. The walls are adorned with paintings done by the Germans, all on propaganda lines, with a lot of skulls and crossbones and warnings of what happens to cowards, the glory of dying for the fatherland and the assets of the super-race. They do really think quite a deal about themselves, but the paintings were very good ones and must have been the work of an expert. Our sanitary man is now removing them with the aid of a Belgian woman and some petrol.

Friday 6 Oct
Beside housing HQ 1 Corps (Main) these barracks are also catering for 'collaborateurs', male and female, political prisoners and two companies of the FBI (*Forces Belges de l'Intérieur*), the local Maquis. The women have their heads shaved and get all the dirty work to do. In squads of twenty or so under an armed guard they wash floors and clean out rooms and even empty the latrines. I don't like to see this, but the FBI say that they are lucky not to have been shot as they had betrayed FBI men to the Germans. Something seems to have gone wrong with the advance, for the first time since Normandy we have stopped. Our divs have been halted by a strong German army on a line five miles north of this

town, stretching from Eindhoven to the Scheldt. This is rather difficult country to keep the ball rolling and favours the defenders.

Saturday 7 Oct
1 Corps are going to do something soon for under command as from today we will have, 3 Armoured Divs, 2 Infantry Divs, 3 Armoured Bdes, 4 AGRA, 77 AA Bde. They are 1 Pol Armd, 4 Cdn Armd, 7 Armd, 33 and 1 Cdn Armd Bdes. With this weight of armour we should be able to sweep right up to Amsterdam. Also the old favourites 49 and 51 (H) Div. There is very little to report on the Corps front. Jerry is sowing mines as fast as he can now that he has a lull and the Engrs are picking them up, but with quite a few casualties for he is using mines that cannot be detected by the normal methods.

Sunday 8 Oct
2 Cdn Inf Div yesterday made a successful seaborne landing in the Scheldt Estuary, their objective being to neutralise enemy guns which are menacing our shipping – well more than that even, preventing our ships from using Antwerp. Until all the Estuary is cleared of the Germans the port will be denied to British ships. This means clearing South Beveland and Walcheren also. The Navy as usual played a magnificent part in the landing operations and the infantry were in by dusk and had secured a good bridge-head by dawn this morning. Casualties are fair.

Monday 9 Oct
First American Army now have Aachen in their grasp and were last heard to be encircling the city; they are right round it except for a gap of 5 miles on the east side. Aachen has been continu-ously bombed by the Lancasters ever since the Americans got their eye on it, so I doubt if there is much left of the place. Still this will be a nasty blow to the German morale for it is one of her main cities this side of the Ruhr. Canadians are enlarging their bridge-head, Second British Army are fighting like madmen in the Arnhem district. It appears that the airborne invasion of that area would have been a complete success but for an atrocious piece of luck. Our intelligence correctly reported that Arnhem was prac-tically free of German troops two days before the operation, but as our men were practically descending 3 crack Panzer Divs were just pulling into Arnhem en route for the Belgian fighting. Had

99

the landing taken place two or three days later there would have been a very different story to tell, but it is just the luck I suppose.* Jerry seems to always have the luck though. I remember back in Normandy if one of our chaps shot a German plane down it was almost certain to drop on a petrol or ammo dump – and the weather so far has been all in the defenders' favour. Our luck will change shortly though.

Tuesday 10 Oct
Our troops (1 Brit Corps) are now well over the Dutch border and 49 Div have relieved Baarle Nassau whilst Second Army elements cleared Eindhoven without much ado. There is a great demand for bridging and under command we have been fortunate to get the 86 Bridging Coy RASC. These br coys are terrific affairs, packing 900 men and 600 vehicles. They carry Bailey bridging for the sappers and are split up into platoons, FBP platoon is the Folding Boat Platoon, then there is the Pontoon Platoon and the Accessory Platoon. Each platoon is called forward as required, but if the job is not handled by an efficient staff officer during an operation then there can be a terrible muck up. It is difficult to have scores of lorries milling around a bridging site without getting them a little out of sequence.

Wednesday 11 Oct
The Americans have closed the gap around Aachen and already have sent in their ultimatum to the commander, but as usual he is a pig-headed Nazi and has turned it down. The Yanks invented their own V1 in the shape of a derelict tramcar which they loaded down with explosive. It was then sent careering down the tramway track, exploding in the city square. Talking of V1s, the Hun has commenced once more his attacks on London, this time from launching platforms in Holland. I'm pleased Mary and the baby are in South Elmsall, both doing well too.† I wonder whether leave will start. Perhaps we will stick it out to the end. This war should be over even now by Christmas.

* Apart from unexpectedly strong forces, unfavourable weather prevented the rapid reinforcement of the airborne troops by the 52nd Lowland Division, and their supply from the air. This might have made all the difference.
† South Elmsall in Yorkshire, and away from the bombing. My mother's family had moved from Kent to Surrey to escape the bombing, but were still not entirely safe.

Thursday 12 Oct
I've been getting a bad opinion of these Belgian underground merchants lolling around this barracks in their comic opera uniforms. In the first place many of them only went underground as we arrived, so as to make a good impression on the British. They appear to be arresting a lot of innocent people too, and closing cafes for no other reason than their own gain. Cafe proprietors are brought before a bench of 5 KLs and accused of charging excessive prices for cognac. Their cafes are then closed, but 4 out of these 5 just men, themselves own cafes. Outside the gates of this Caserne stands a long queue of friends and relatives. They wait all day long in the hope of seeing one of the prisoners. They are never allowed to visit, but if they wait long enough they will perhaps see their friend either going to work or being escorted to the latrines. The FBI gentleman on the gate treats them in a very offhand manner and some of our chaps have expressed their disgust at the way he pushes the old ladies around. I can see a spot of bother cropping up if we stay here much longer. Our defence company are pretty tough eggs.

Friday 13 Oct
The war is now definitely slowing down. The Cdns in the Scheldt are having to fight for every inch of ground, we are making no use of the armour in 1 Corps as I expected and – horror of horrors – we are mine laying. This means defensive warfare. I can't understand it. In the meantime though our divs are consolidating behind these minefields. Perhaps there will be another grand offensive soon, although we are doing no planning for one. I get quite a bit of time off these days and as we have an army cinema unit in town quite a pleasant evening can be spent. The shops have little or nothing in them; what they have is out of the reach of the soldier. A pair of artificial silk stockings can be bought for the equivalent of £3.10s.

Saturday 14 Oct
The Germans had a novel way of raising money for their troops in Belgium. They just rolled off on their own presses as much as they needed. The poor Belgians were forced to accept this spurious money. Consequently the prices soared to the skies. The higher they soared the more money the Germans printed, so they were always on the right side. Now the big crack has occurred. The Belgian government are issuing a new 100 franc note, all the

old notes of this denomination are null and void. Nobody can change more than 2000 francs, so if the Belgian hasn't got his money in a bank then he has lost it. There is definitely going to be a spot of bother between the Government and the people soon, but this is not our concern. Three Germans were arrested in town today, soldiers in civilian uniform. According to law they can be shot as spies. They were brought here this afternoon looking a little ashamed of themselves as an angry crowd escorted them down the street laughing and jeering and spitting on them.

Sunday 15 Oct
All six armies now lined up against the Germans are at a standstill except the 7th which landed from Italy. They are closing the Belfort Gap, but even they are finding the going a little tough. We were today treated to a splendid show of military when the Canadian Army Military Band played this afternoon in the Market Square in Turnhout. The Flems gave them a great ovation. It is a very good band indeed and I am sure that the martial music was good for all morales concerned.

Monday 16 Oct
Last night I heard a sound which I last heard whilst sitting outside Caen. It was unmistakable – the V1 or flying bomb. There were three in all and they were en route for Antwerp. This is the only sound of war I have heard since I arrived at this location, but life here is rather monotonous. We are spitting and polishing once more. Continually working indoors has robbed me of the healthy look I had of but a few weeks ago. I wish we were moving up front again sometimes, just to get stuck in and get the war over with. The excitement of being near the Germans, the barrages, the DRs rushing in with vital news, surprises galore, all this made the time whizz by, but this awful standstill that has befallen us is torture. All the time we are still the Hun is reorganising as fast an only the Hun can reorganise – he is laying mines and digging in. It will soon be November and I don't fancy a winter campaign in either Belgium or Holland.

Tuesday 17 Oct
The Poles report a slight push to the north of Antwerp. Their opponents are a new div, the 1043 Grenadier Div, newly formed of either men between 40 and 50 or 17 and 20. Cdns also are

fanning out on their bridgehead, but there is nothing really of importance to note on the whole Corps front.

Wednesday 18 Oct
A new American div has now come under the command of 1 Corps. It is the 104 (Timberwolves) Division and this is their baptism of fire. The commander has stated that they are simply itching to get their teeth into the enemy, but perhaps Jerry will make these Timberwolves howl a bit. He's rather more used to fighting then they are. We've had to let 51 (H) Div go and 7 Armd also, so we've made a pretty bad swap I'm thinking. They (104) will take up a position on the Dutch border opposite Breda.

Thursday 19 Oct
During the night one of the women prisoners tried to make a break for it. They are quartered in the top storey of the barracks, so she tied her blankets together and began to lower herself down, but as the strong blankets were only connected with weak string she didn't get very far before they broke. She fell 30 feet to her death. Yanks have told the Germans in Aachen to surrender or else . . . but of course Jerry turned their recommendations down.

Friday 20 Oct
Still all quiet on the Corps front and even we are no longer busy. Life has now taken on the air of soldiering in England – just the same conditions, parades, rifle inspections, trousers creased, gaiters blancoed etc. The Quartermaster is very liberal with his issues just now. The Americans turned all their full artillery on Aachen and the RAF Lancasters deposited another 2000 tons. After this the Yanks captured the place. They were fired on by boys of 14 years old. The underground, it appears, in German cities is a very strong formation.

Saturday 21 Oct
The Corps Commander's son, a Capt in the RAC, was on a recce in the Breda area. His armoured car was fired on and he was killed. This must be a bitter blow for the 'old man', for until recently his son was his personal ADC. The Corps Commander hasn't shown any signs of being upset and has even distributed his son's kit to his batman and driver. Lt General Sir John Crocker, KBE, CB, DSO, MC Commander 1 Corps is a soldier to the backbone. He directed 1 Corps operations very successfully

and got quite a build up in the *Tatler* recently. His escapades with the British First Army in North Africa were miraculous and always during active ops he is in the thick of it like his master Gen Montgomery.

Sunday 22 Oct
Today General Montgomery visited the Corps Commander and a conference was held. I saw all the Div commanders arrive in all their splendour, the Pole looking the most splendid of them all. Monty had 4 out-riders, big fine military police with their equipment blancoed white, also a jeep with four more burly policemen in it, all with their sub-machine guns at the alert. Monty stepped out of his Rolls Royce wearing white corduroy trousers and a fur-lined airman's jacket. Immediately his hands were in his pockets and he looked the most unsoldierly of them all. Still, he's the brains behind it all so he can be excused. I hope that they get things cracking on our front, even if they put us back into the front line.*

Monday 23 Oct
British Second Army did a bit of good bridging last night and today their famous 50 Div were battling their way towards Tilburg in Holland, 2 Cdn Corps pushed out from their bridgehead towards Bergen-op-Zoom also in Holland, whilst the Poles are drawing nigh to Breda. It looks as though we are at last beginning to find a way through the elaborate German defences. Our 4 Cdn Armd Div captured Brasschaet north of Antwerp and almost on the Dutch border. They have caused quite a rout in the German ranks.

Tuesday 24 Oct
Quite a surprise today when we suddenly moved to Camp de Brasschaet which is still hot from the battle of yesterday. Like our last billet, signs of the SS are everywhere. Their insignia are painted on all the walls and some of the paintings are really very well done. We have to do quite a deal of cleaning up here, for this

---

* As a result of this meeting, 1st British Corps with 49th Division, 104th U.S. Division, the Polish and 4th Canadian Armoured Divisions were charged with the task of clearing the area of Holland west of Nijmegen and south of the river Maas towards the Tilburg – Breda – Bergen-op-Zoom.

place was taken and retaken twice before the Germans decided to evacuate. The countryside is very flat and uninteresting and the village nearby has suffered quite a deal of damage. There are more cafes here than houses and already some of them are out of bounds to troops. Our MO says that 80% of the women in this area suffer from VD. This sounds like an exaggeration, but it is a known fact that German divs in the Balkans were afflicted by this malady in a big way and then transferred to this front to end their unhappy days for the Fatherland.

Wednesday 25 Oct
This area comes under the hammer of the V1 and V2 it appears and they are coming over in convoy en route to Antwerp. They fly so low that the very walls of this building shudder with the vibrations. All of them don't carry on to the port, some decide to park themselves nearby and not at all gently. Our divs are now steadily pushing into Holland. 49 Div are in the news again with a nice thrust towards Roosendaal, which lies on the main lateral running from East to West of southern Holland. There will be heavy fighting right up to the Maas, for the RAF have destroyed all the bridges and Jerry is trying to stave us off until he can construct new ones – or get enough ferrying material to get his army back.

Thursday 26 Oct
The V2 is a horrible weapon and is on the Rocket principle. The 'I' (*Information?*) people tell us that it is 46' long, 5'8" wide with fins of 16". It carries 6,000 lbs of high explosive and is launched from bases in North Holland. It travels upwards at 3,500 miles an hour for a distance of 65 miles, on its downward journey its speed is reduced to 2,500 mph. The explosion and blast effect is not quite as bad as that of the V1, because it hits the ground with such force that most of the explosion occurs below ground level. There is very little warning of its approach and it can travel 400 miles. Already we have had two in this district. Some civilians and troops were killed.

Friday 27 Oct
British Second Army have captured Tilburg in a lightning thrust, the final strike being made by the 15th Scottish Division. This is quite a large town with about 80,000 population. A flying bomb today gave us a rare shaking up but it dropped in an open field.

There is a POW camp close to us and just now it is rather packed with gentlemen of the super race. I see the MPs searching the prisoners. They look a motley crowd, some with beards and some with no boots. I bet they haven't tasted such food as they are getting now, for they get the same rations as we do, and we now get lovely white bread and fresh rations three times a week.

Saturday 28 Oct
Our Polish Armoured Division today captured Breda, a very historical Dutch town on the main southern lateral. They got it without much ado, so that puts two important towns in our hands. I think the Germans are beginning to break up a little under our increasing pressure. He doesn't quite know whether to stay and fight or get back over the Maas whilst the going is good. Well, today we said goodbye to our Timberwolf friends. They weren't given the chance to get their teeth into the Hun as they desired but were given a full time job on road maintenance and keeping bridges up to scratch. They are probably a good div when they feel their feet. Just now ours is the quietest front of them all, so that is perhaps why Gen Eisenhower had them broken in with us. Their infantry came up against a small German counter-attack between the Poles and 49 Div sectors and Jerry knocked 3 miles out of the Yanks, but 49 soon straightened out the bulge.

*2nd Lt Walter Horne remembered this unit well. At a Duke of Wellington's Group meeting, "we were informed that a 'green' Allied Division was to be blooded during the action between October 19th and November 3rd, which culminated in the capture of Roosendaal. The Dukes attacked and we gained our objective. The 'green' Division was then ordered to attack an objective in front of our position. The officer commanding the formation which passed through my platoon said, 'Not to worry lads, we'll get there', which indeed they did. However, after a short period of time they withdrew through our positions again, remarking in passing, 'It's too ****** warm up there!' The result was that we had to advance from our position which we had consolidated to re-take the position which they had evacuated! We later found that it was an American Division nicknamed the 'Wolf' Division which later went on to prove its worth."*

Sunday 29 Oct
The 49th West Riding Division today captured Roosendaal but are still having minor troubles with nests of snipers.

The Yorkshire Pud has much to say on this. The Duke of Wellington's Regiment was sent to take the large anti-tank ditch which surrounded the town. 'C' Company had to cross a ditch and advance 800 yards over open fen. The Company was sniped so that, "It was only possible to crawl, and where crawling was possible one crawled in water. 'B' Company spent a most uncomfortable day pinned down in water ditches by close range sniping and mortaring. 'D' Company protected our right flank and wholly engaged the enemy's attention by . . . very gallant patrols and raids". (Op. cit. p. 14) It was here that 2nd Lt Horne won his Military Cross by evacuating every man of his platoon from an exposed position, passing twice through a minefield, under heavy fire.

When the Regiment finally entered Roosendaal, they received an ecstatic welcome.

Canadians captured Bergen-op-Zoom so that now puts the whole of the southern lateral in our hands. From reports the DRs gave us of these Dutch towns they are pretty barren but the people are giving our boys a terrific ovation. Seems that the people are either all for us or else very much against us, as the Dutch formed a whole SS Division for the German army.

In June, 1940, Himmler had authorized the enlistment of Dutch and Belgian volunteers into the SS Regiment 'Westland'. More 'foreign legions' were set up as part of the Waffen-SS in July, 1941, including Dutch, Belgian, Danish and Norwegian volunteers. They later served on the Russian front. Two Dutch divisions were to be set up in 1945.

More Vs 1 and 2 in this area. The American First Army reinforced by the Timberwolves are now slowly advancing along the Aachen–Cologne road, the 7th Army are through the Belfort Gap with the French under Gen Leclerc fighting extremely well.

Monday 30 Oct
Although we have the port of Antwerp Jerry is still denying us the use of it for he has the Scheldt well covered with his big guns

on Walcheren and South Beveland and until these two islands are over-run no shipping can get up to the port. 2 Cdn Corps have got this job in hand and I notice that they have recently taken under their command 32 Assault Regt RE – our Le Havre heroes.* I think they will stage a landing soon.

Tuesday 31 Oct
Our Divs are now sweeping forward towards the Maas from a line, Tilburg – Breda – Roosendaal – Bergen-op-Zoom and yesterday the engineers constructed 6 Bailey bridges. We still have plenty of bridging equipment in reserve, thanks to the foresight of Brig Campbell DSO MC our Chief Engineer, who by the way bid us goodbye on the 26th as he left for Second Army as Chief Engineer. He was a very trying man and a driver to the officers. His temper wasn't too good and he would often stamp and shout and swear about the most trivial matters, but the fact remained that he was very efficient and got massive jobs done in record time. Our new CE Brig H.E. Pike DSO, seems to be a very nice man and he interviewed us each in turn as soon as he arrived. He is only very small and is under the MOs supervision as he had his neck broken in Normandy when his jeep ran over a small mine.

Wednesday 1 Nov
All today Jerry has been plastering this area with his secret weapons and I thought that sooner or later he would register a bullseye. It arrived this afternoon, like a bolt from the blue and I thought the end of the world had come with it. I've never experienced an explosion like this one during the whole campaign. Four civilians were killed and 3 of our MPs severely injured. My left ear seized up on me again, but as I have still one left there is no need to go to the MO about it. 52 (Lowland) Div under command 2 Cdn Corps with 42 Assault Regt RE today made a seaborne landing on Walcheren and from recent reports they are doing well on their first assignment. They went in without air support because the weather was too bad, but the Navy provided good covering fire from two monitors and the *Warspite*. This ship I

---

* By this stage, the Canadians and Lowlanders had completely linked up on South Beveland at the conclusion of Operation Vitality, thus cutting off Walcheren.

think has fought the war itself by the amount of jobs it has been mixed up in.*

41st, 47th and 48th Royal Marine Commandos of the 4th Special Service Brigade also landed on Walcheren on 1 November. Of twenty-five landing craft of the support squadron carrying rockets and light artillery, nine were sunk and eleven put out of action while drawing fire away from the commandos. The island was ten square miles, the greatest part being under sea level. Its defences included minefields, beach obstacles, anti-tank and anti-airborne obstacles, concrete emplacements for artillery and automatic weapons, flame-throwers and coastal guns. The whole was surrounded by dykes. The R.E. AVREs suffered dreadful casualties against such defences. "Under heavy fire the four landing craft carrying the assault teams of 79th Division followed up. One was hit repeatedly, the small box girder bridge was shot away from its AVRE, and an AVRE carrying a fascine set on fire. A second was hit astern and had many casualties and had to withdraw and come in later. It eventually appeared to the right of the other craft and landed its load all but one Crab which was in-extricably mixed up in the wreckage of the bridge which had been destroyed by enemy fire. But its bulldozer, in an attempt to rescue a foundered AVRE from another craft, sank in a quicksand. It was from a third that the foundered AVRE had emerged, its bridge AVRE being hit by a shell. From the fourth the two Crabs stuck in the mud when one attempted to pull the other out, but the bridge AVRE disembarked, laid its bridge successfully over some bad going, and then crossing got bogged in the exit, blocking the way for the second AVRE which was following it closely and both were drowned by the rising tide." (Pakenham-Walsh, Op. cit., p 419) It must have been a nightmare. And yet in spite of such bad luck, the landing was successful and the objective, Westkapelle, was captured that first day.

At the same time, the 155th Infantry Brigade of 52nd (L) Division with No. 4 Commando Battalion landed at Flushing.

Thursday 2 Nov
52 (L) Div have already cleared ¾ of Walcheren and captured Middelburg the largest town. 250 British infantry men got the surprise of their lives when they entered Middelburg and found

---

* Although the fog in England also grounded the spotter planes which were supposed to direct their fire, so the warships made little impression on the German batteries.

1500 squareheads sitting in the market square awaiting capture. The Garrison Commander had got a severe toothache and was so incapacitated that he had no heart for the fight.

There is some confusion in my father's account of the Walcheren campaign and I sense that he must have been writing up several days' events at once, some time after they occurred. Flushing was almost cleared by 52nd (L) Division on 2 November (though the German Command Post in the Hotel Britannia took an extra day).

The surrender of Middelburg actually came later, on 6 November. A Company of the 7th/9th Royal Scots had to navigate the floodwaters into Middelburg in Buffaloes (tracked amphibian carriers), taking the garrison by surprise. There was little resistance. Major Johnston, the Commanding Officer, negotiated the surrender with the Garrison Commander, Lieut.-Gen. Daser of the 70th Division. There was a 'toothache' rumour, but in his History of the 52nd (Lowland) Division *George Blake notes "that Daser had been relying to a considerable extent on Dutch courage and was inclined to behave like a sulky infant." (Jackson Son and Co. Glasgow 1950 p. 112) Certainly Daser could not bring himself to surrender to a mere Major of the Royal Scots. A temporary promotion to Lieut.-Col. for the Scots officer satisfied the General's honour.*

All the surrounding countryside has been inundated to a depth of about a yard by the Hun. Land that the Dutch have fought for for 50 years against the sea has now been rendered useless by these swine who blew breaches in the dykes and let in the sea water onto arable land, not the least advantage to the Germans but depriving a lot of the Dutch people of their homes and livelihood.* Our chaps made the Germans stand up and left them there in a blizzard for 24 hours - because there was nowhere to put them?

About 3,000 German prisoners were held by 200 British troops in the town square for several tense hours. Many of them had surrendered against their will and the situation was further complicated when some Dutch citizens chose to take the opportunity to settle old scores by

* 37,000 Dutch civilians were stranded in the upper storeys of their flooded homes in Middelburg. However, he has placed all the blame perhaps unfairly on the Germans. For three weeks before the invasion the R.A.F. bombed the dykes, blowing four great gaps through which the sea rushed, flooding the interior of the island. Only the dunes and dykes remained above water, which was of course tidal.

110

loosing off stolen rifles. The situation calmed down when reinforcements finally arrived. Meanwhile, the Garrison Commander was kept occupied with another bottle of champagne.

There was no snow during the whole of the Walcheren campaign, but no doubt the image of a dejected, humiliated garrison standing for hours in a blizzard spiced up the rumour.

Friday 3 Nov
47 Royal Marine Commandos made a seaborne landing on South Beveland (Walcheren?) and without many casualties captured Flushing, but Flushing can hardly be called a port any more for it has been severely demolished by the retreating Hun. But why did he leave Antwerp? We wouldn't use Flushing as a port anyway. Now that we have Antwerp we have everything our hearts desire by way of ports. Poor old 49 div engineers got a pasting last night whilst doing a bridging operation. They lost two bridges and the best part of two sections from a sudden heavy artillery barrage. They are getting a little too close to the Hun to do serious bridging. What is required is hasty bridging just yet.

Saturday 4 Nov
Walcheren is now in our hands and South Beveland soon will be.*
These are both masterstrokes for now Antwerp can be used without interference except from E boats (*German naval attack boats*) and 1 man submarines. 52 (L) div have done excellent work on their first job. It seems rather ironical that this Div should have a shoulder flash 'Mountain' and spend four years in Scotland training as mountain troops – expert mountaineers – and their first job takes place on an island so flat that it is 20' below sea level. Still, that's the army all over.

The 52nd Lowland Division trained in the winter with the Norwegians, learning how to ski, to use sledges and huskies, and to survive in extreme conditions. But they also trained in the summer with Indians, learning how to get the best out of the terrain, how to use mules for transport, and again, survival. They practised seaborne landings (at Inverary) as well as airborne assaults. So they were much more than expert mountaineers.

On the 25th of last month a civilian got to our lines and gave

* These two should be the other way round.

111

us the location of the German Army (15th) HQ. The Corps Comd put the Typhoons of 84 Gp on it and now we have discovered that the whole of the HQ staff, about 50 officers, were caught in conference. As the building was rocketed I doubt if many got away alive. The German Air Force was active over all the fronts yesterday and a total of 208 planes were shot down. I had occasion to go with Lt Baird through Antwerp today and en route we had quite a narrow squeak. A V1 crashed on the main road about 400 yds ahead of us – another minute would have done it. Unlucky at cards but lucky at flying bombs. Antwerp doesn't seem to be showing much signs of damage, although there was quite a deal of glass in the streets. The people were carrying on as though there was nothing to worry about. I didn't go much on the place.

Sunday 5 Nov
Our divs are smashing the 15th German Army back to the Maas on a wide front. Our RAF have smashed most of the bridges although there is a very fine crossing at the Moerdyk – a road bridge and railway bridge. We won't touch these for as things are we might even beat Jerry to them. It he gets there first he will most certainly destroy them. The weather is rather bad just now, but although this grounds our Air Force it makes no difference to the V1s. We had a couple of close ones today and they made the glass splinter somewhat. 2 Cdn Corps, 52 (L) Div have cleared Walcheren except for a few fanatical snipers. The commandos report that Flushing is beyond hasty repair, but that doesn't matter much as we can now commence unloading in Antwerp. L of C troops, mainly pioneers and RE Works Coys have the clearing up of the docks, then some more RE take over – Docks Operating Coys. I think the RE seem to be doing everything these days. The only job badly done is the Postal Service.

Monday 6 Nov
The whole of 9 Coy of the 3 Battalion 1 Brigade, 1063 Grenadier Regt deserted to our lines today, including the OC. They tell of atrocities committed by the SS north of the Maas. This company has only been formed about a month and came to this front straight from Leipzig. They were quickly sick of the fighting and the bullying methods of the SS and Gestapo. They told tales of atrocities committed on the Dutch by the SS and said that the bragging SS made rape hackneyed talk. The Gestapo have

threatened reprisals on soldiers' families in the case of desertion. In the case of retreat in the face of the enemy the Gestapo shoot down the German soldiers unmercifully – nice fellows the Gestapo. Himmler seems to be the big boss nowadays and with his Special Police, rules with an iron hand.

Chapter Nine

The Winter Battle for the Maas and the Ardennes Offensive

Eisenhower's plan for the autumn of 1944 had been to gain the line of the River Rhine, or at least to meet and destroy the German armies to the west of the river. While Montgomery had concentrated on opening up Antwerp, further south, the American 1st and 3rd Armies had been fighting to capture ground around Aachen and in Lorraine. During November the U.S. 1st and 9th Armies broke through the West Wall (Siegfried Line) into the Hurtgen Forest and pressed on to the River Roer. Patton and the 3rd U.S. Army pushed through Lorraine, reaching the line of the Rhine and the West Wall by mid-December. Further north, the British and Canadians had pushed to the line of the Maas by early November, but the push had sunk into an autumn stalemate, the German defenders being helped by the weather, rivers, floods and mud. Eisenhower's strategy had not worked partly because the various moves had not been made in sufficient strength. Attacks had been made in too many places at once. In early December, the German front was still intact.

Against this background was played out Hitler's bold attempt to drive two Panzer armies (6th SS and 5th Panzer) through the Ardennes forests and across the Meuse to seize Antwerp, 100 miles away. Codenamed Operation "Autumn Mist", it was also designed to separate the British and Canadians in the north from the Americans in the south, spread confusion, and give Hitler time to deal a knock-out blow against the Russians who were advancing towards Berlin. The point chosen for the attack was weakly held by U.S. divisions which were either inexperienced or resting. The offensive came as a complete surprise, because, although signs of an impending attack had been spotted, they had been misinterpreted. No-one expected an attack in such a formidable location.

On the morning of 16 December the Germans quickly overran the American defenders. Eisenhower's reaction was to send armoured and airborne troops to hold the vital road junctions of St Vith and Bastogne, while reserves were rushed up from other sectors. St Vith was lost but Bastogne held out, despite being completely surrounded, until it was relieved by Patton's 4th Armoured Division on 26 December.

On 20 December Montgomery took command of American troops to the north of the 'bulge', and with 30 Corps, pushed home his counter-attack, while Patton did the same from the south. Meanwhile, an improvement in the weather allowed Allied air operations to resume on 23 December. A desperate shortage of petrol complicated German problems. In spite of his protests, Hitler would not allow Von Rundstedt to withdraw. Montgomery's major counter-attack on the 'bulge' came on 3 January. By the 7th, the Germans were becoming trapped with only one supply route, the Houffalize road. By the 8th, permission was granted to begin the withdrawal.

In all, the Wehrmacht lost 120,000 casualties, 600 tanks and 1600 aircraft. Allied casualties were 76,000. The drive into Germany had been set back by six weeks. At its deepest, the 'bulge' had pushed forward 70 miles. By 26 January most of the ground had been recaptured.

During the Ardennes offensive, there was a fear that the Germans would counter-attack in Holland also, and the Breda garrison had been put on full alert. The threat subsided as the 'bulge' was pushed back, but one isolated German garrison that held out through all this was on the island of Kapelsche Veer in the mouth of the River Maas. Several attempts were made to capture the garrison, but not until the end of January was a combined Armoured–Royal Engineer effort successful.

While the Russians pressed in from the East in their dash to Berlin, the diary finishes abruptly with the unfolding of Eisenhower's Rhineland plan, whereby, on 8 February, 30 British Corps under the 1st Canadian Army, attacked the Reichswald Forest, south east of Nijmegen, in Operation Veritable. This led to a fierce and sustained resistance as the Wehrmacht tried to keep the Rhine open as Germany's main supply route.

Tuesday 7 Nov
Our francs were today changed to guilders and off we set to Tilburg relieved a week last Friday by the 15 (S) Div of Second Brit Army. This is quite a large town with a population of about 100,000. The town has never been bombed by either the Germans or us. It never came under our shellfire even when it was captured. The German defenders were beaten before the town and retreated through it as fast as their stolen bicycles, prams and anything else on wheels that didn't require petrol to propel it, could carry them. The people are very friendly and gave us quite an ovation even so long after they have been liberated. These proud Dutch are in a bad way though for food and clothing. The main streets of Tilburg have some very nice shops but they are all empty, emptier than any other shops I have seen in towns of France and Belgium.

Wednesday 8 Nov
We are billeted in the Kazerne, which was only completed in 1939. It is a magnificent barracks and was the HQ of an SS Div. Before the Germans left they set it on fire, but only the entrance is damaged as the Dutch resistance put the fire out after the SS beat it. There are now 64 German Divs in the North of Holland. Some of these have come from Finland and some from Norway. A lot of the 15th German Army have been slaughtered on the Maas but I believe the majority of them have been got across. The weather was too much against our fellows. Roosevelt was today re-elected. The Dutch claim the President of America as one of their countrymen, Roosevelt meaning 'Field of Roses'. I'll never learn this terrible garble of a language. Perhaps I won't have much need for what few Dutch I have met seem to be able to speak English. It is the principal foreign language taught in Dutch schools. There has been no schooling or studying in Holland since the invasion began.*

Thursday 9 Nov
Of our divs the Poles are the first to reach the Maas proper and are wondering how they are going to cross. Pro-tem they are halted. There has been no planning about what we do when we cross the Maas. 49 Div have gone to Second Army and so we have

---

* The universities closed down, but the schools managed to continue.

now only the Poles and 4 Cdn Armd Div to administer unto. Cdns didn't beat the Germans to the Moerdyk bridges. Well they may have done, but when the SS were across the Germans blew both bridges and left quite a goodly number of their Wehrmacht on this side. They are now throwing up their hands wholesale, but it's the Cdns they are facing.

Friday 10 Nov
All fronts are now once more at a standstill and the Russians also. 'Germany Calling' [Lord Haw Haw's broadcasts] is bragging about Fortress Germany and how her magnificent troops have halted the Allies on all fronts. Very little is happening in Italy. Soon they will be claiming a major victory for this temporary stoppage of the steam roller. We are not very busy and I have time occasionally to walk into Tilburg which is about a mile away. I made the acquaintance of one Jan Pijnenburg, a reputed cyclist and world champion 6 day rider. He is very good to me and seems to have suffered very little during the occupation owing to the vast wealth he accumulated during his successful years as a professional. He has a very good class cafe, but he has nothing to sell.* He could always buy what he wanted on the Black Market, mainly from the Germans, who charged the equivalent of 10/– for a loaf of black bread and £1 for 20 cigarettes of decent quality. Now the British are at it and a bottle of whisky can be bought for £12, a tablet of soap for 6/–. The soldiers themselves don't get this price but they sell to a Black Marketeer who in turn sells to the rich. Holland before the war was a very rich country. They stood little chance with their old-fashioned army when the Germans entered without a word of warning, but the Dutch Resistance movement has been the best of all occupied countries and they have wreaked havoc amongst the German troops, but they have always had to pay dearly in hostages. It is said that 30,000 Dutchmen have been killed since the occupation.

Saturday 11 Nov
British Second Army are today in the news. They have launched

---

* In 1991 we visited Holland to trace the later stages of the diary. In Tilburg, we met people who could well remember the 'Old Dutch Cafe', and who knew the Pijnenburg family. We spoke to his daughter via an interpreter, but Mr Pijnenburg had died three months earlier.

a large-scale attack between Nijmegen and Aachen and are heading for a German town just over the border but in front of the Siegfried Line – Geilenkirchen. They have made quite good progress today. The old 3 Brit Inf Div with 5 Aslt RE as a spearhead are leading the attack. Just after they put their attack under way the weather cracked up and the rain is simply teeming down. This is hard luck for that ground is boggy at the best of time.

Sunday 12 Nov
The rain is still pouring down and already our engineers are having to lay Sommerfeld tracking. The roads have turned to rivers and this flat country can't take such a deluge. It would be an impossibility to try and move tanks in this.* I think that this country will slip back into the sea altogether soon, what with the weight of Jerry's 64 Divs and our two armies. Somebody will have to get off or else we will all go under with it. Although we have recognised 64 German Divs north of the Maas this is not so bad as it sounds, for a German Div of today can be as low as 3,000 men. Still, the lower they are the better. These Huns are tough, but they have every reason to be. They are fighting with their backs to the Fatherland and I am convinced had they landed in England in '40, then we also would have fought just as fanatically and just as well.

Monday 13 Nov
Second Army are still pushing ahead and reports from their sappers on mineclearance are very interesting. With the roads in such a bad state the Hun knew that 2 Army would have to do a lot of maintenance, so convenient piles of hardcore and gravel were booby-trapped, so that the first time they were disturbed there was a terrific explosion. Then the old dodge of using our signs 'Verges Cleared to 10" were laid everywhere. The sappers met Schumines, Glassmines, Picric Pot, Tellers with push-pull igniters, earthernware and dummies. This slowed up the advance a good deal. All bomb craters were extensively mined so that the bulldozers were rendered useless, trees lying across the road were booby-trapped and houses purposely left intact and inviting – to anybody but the wary.

* The weather was hindering the use of air power also.

Tuesday 14 Nov

The RAF recently located and wiped out a number of V1 sites in northern Holland. They also demolished vital bridges over which the Germans had to transport their V2s to launching bases, so recently we have been free of these pests. Three Germans in British uniform were arrested in Tilburg today. They are suspected of being on a sabotage errand and said they were officer cadets of the 116 Panzer Div. They admitted the difficulty with which they were confronted all the time and that was our extensive 'guard' system. They were rowed across the Maas and were due back tomorrow night. There will be three absentees when the roll is called up yonder. Our divs are minelaying and sending nightly patrols over the Maas.

Wednesday 15 Nov

During the occupation, the Dutch saved numerous British and American airmen from the Germans. These they passed by under-ground to Belgium whilst we were there, but some stayed in Tilburg until we arrived. It can easily be imagined how difficult it was to even feed these refugees let alone hide them, for the rationing under the Germans was very meagre, being only 1500 calories per person per day. This was 500 calories under the necessary to keep a normal human fit and well. Collaborateurs sold their fellow countrymen to the Germans by telling the Gestapo where these pilots were hiding. One woman had 5 RAF boys hidden for 3 months and a shopkeeper became suspicious as she tried to buy bread at a Black price. For a nominal sum he told the Gestapo. These 'beestmannen' first of all went to the wrong house but without asking any questions they machine-gunned a man and his wife. They searched and found nothing. Eventually they found the right house and killed the RAF boys and the woman in cold blood. These were the Green Police and their names have been recorded for the day of reckoning. The collaborator tried to escape with the Germans when we arrived, but they didn't want him anymore. He got left behind and was strangled by the Dutch Underground. His body lay in the gutter when our men entered. The Dutch have made a fine grave for the airmen and it is well kept.

Thursday 16 Nov

American First Army commanded by that excellent General (in my opinion, their best) General Hodges, is now breaking away

119

from Aachen and are on the road to Cologne. The British Second Army with elements of the American 9th today shared the honour of, firstly obliterating and then capturing Geilenkirchen. The town is supposed to be finished altogether. We don't mind. This is how it should be with all German cities that hold out. We didn't like to knock the French towns about, but we don't mind what we do to the Germans. If they don't give up a city then we just put the Lancs on them.

Geilenkirchen was situated on the Siegfried Line where Montgomery's Second Army joined Bradley's 9th U.S. Army. Whereas attacks elsewhere had been thwarted by a shortage of ammunition and muddy ground which hindered the use of armour, this was a notable success. The defences of the Siegfried Line were intact here, but the defenders could not withstand the heavy and concentrated artillery power available to the combined British and American forces.

The incursion on German soil had a great effect on morale, as my father's diary entry suggests. Lieut.-Col. J.F.D. Savage, C.R.E., 42nd Assault Regiment reported to his Brigade commander on arriving with his AVREs on German soil, "Henceforth petarding will be indulged in with added zest and vigour". (Pakenham-Walsh, Op. cit. p. 442)

Friday 17 Nov
6 Allied armies are now pounding the Germans on their own doorstep, but even so the Hun is sticking to his guns. Gen LeClerc of the French 1 Army has promised the Germans that for every French soldier killed by German resistance movements 10 German hostages will be shot also. Underground fighters are *not* soldiers and are treated as spies. They wear no uniform or distinguishing emblem to denote that they are in the war and so have a soldier at a disadvantage. This is the sort of measure the French are expected to adopt and I hope we and the Americans do likewise, but the Yanks haven't made much effort to stamp it out behind their lines in the Aachen area. Resisters are playing havoc with the American lines of communication. Wire ropes are hung across main roads and in the dark a DR can get his head chopped off. This has actually happened to the Americans. For the Fatherland, these Huns will fight to the last gasp.

Saturday 18 Nov
Sir Trafford Leigh-Mallory, the man behind the RAF, is missing as he was travelling to Asia to take up command there. His wife was with him too and there has been no news of their plane which is now 3 days overdue.* 52 (L) Div has got a full-time job on Walcheren, evacuating civilians, draining the floods, clearing minefields, constructing roads. Their commander has sent an urgent request for waterproof clothing for civilians and food also as the Dutch are lending a willing hand without even being asked. They require this food and clothing to be able to carry on with the good work. This is no work for an operational div though, and I think that L of C troops will soon take over the admin of this island.

Sunday 19 Nov
This rain is ceaseless and our tanks are sinking as they stand. The RAF is grounded. The Second Army attack has been brought to a standstill by this weather. I bet Brig Campbell is having a few headaches with his road maintenance programme, but he'll drive those sappers through it. He gets jobs done. This semi-static warfare on 1 Corps front is very disheartening and I can see us sticking here right through the winter. It is impossible to attack across the Maas from our sector for all the ground above the river has been inundated. The Hun has blown all the locks. We get a number of line-crossers daily and I believe they pay German soldiers to let them by. They sometimes finish up on our minefields.

Monday 20 Nov
Himmler is now forming the German Home Guard. Do or die tactics are instilled into these over 60 men, which he calls the Volkssturm. This is a good indication of the shortage of manpower which is now confronting the Germans. Hitler has been unheard of for quite a long time now, and Rundstedt whom he sacked after the Normandy debacle now supersedes Model in the west and is once more in command.† Rommel was actually

* Commander in Chief of the Allied Air Forces for the Invasion, he had been appointed Commander in Chief of South-East Asia Command but was killed in an air crash while en route.
† "The conduct of operations since his return in September had been so efficient and successful that Allied Intelligence assumed von Rundstedt was no longer obliged to listen to 'intuitions from afar'". *The Struggle for Europe* by Chester Wilmot, Collins, London, 1952, p. 574.

killed in Normandy when the Typhoons straffed his staff car. He is supposed to have broken his neck and died quickly afterwards, so the German radio announces.* Maurice Chevalier and Charles Carpentier both accused of collaborating with the Germans, have been exonerated from blame. But the French are killing off the 'broken reeds' as quickly as they guillotined the aristocracy in 1789 – it doesn't take them long to try and behead the wrong-doers. There is a spot of bother in Brussels just now because the government is wanting to disarm the Maquis. The Maquis take a poor view of this and so armoured patrols of British troops are in the streets. The Belgians have made a proper muck up of this business.

Tuesday 21 Nov
The French 1 Army along with the American 7th are now making a push towards the Belfort Gap. This Gap will take a lot of hard fighting for it is ideal for the defenders. The French have been held up for quite some time, so let's hope that this push will see them through. Our front is still quite quiet, apart from a few armed patrols at night. The Germans must be nicely settled in north of the Maas by now and when the big attack does come we can expect some extensive minefields to break through. The Germans though must be finding a lot of difficulty with their supply problems for the Dutch are still out on strike and none of the railways are functioning.

Wednesday 22 Nov
In good weather the French yesterday caused a surprise for they pushed up through the Gap and to within 18 miles of Strasbourg. This is really excellent work, for I was afraid the Gap would hold them indefinitely. They have been using French Moroccan troops in this battle and it appears that this type of fighting is very suited to them. Deserters keep trickling across the Maas and they seem willing enough to talk too. In this way our intelligence people can construct the German Order of Battle.

---

* When Rommel was implicated in the July bomb plot, he was given the choice by Hitler of standing trial, with the inherent danger to his family, or committing suicide. He chose poison, but was given a state funeral, having, it was announced, died of his wounds.

Thursday 23 Nov
Yesterday's good news from the French has today been super-seded by the most astounding report that the French have captured Strasbourg intact and by-passed Mulhaus. In our sector the rains are once more deciding our battles and future policy. Holland is one big quagmire and an offensive by anybody in this country is entirely out of the question.

Friday 24 Nov
The French are keeping up the good work and have captured a bridge over the Rhine at Strasbourg. Already they have got across their armoured elements and are consolidating for the next big push. The rain has now reached such proportions in this area that the canals rose 4'9" in 12 hours. We are having two hourly reports on the situation and the sappers are standing by in case of emergency. The whole country will be inundated if this rain doesn't ease up. The German positions must be swamped out too, for they are in country 12' below sea level.*

Saturday 25 Nov
Brit Second Army are engaged in heavy fighting once more, beyond the Maas in their sector. The Germans have some very good positions in the Siegfried Line and we are using Wasps † and Crocodiles (flame-throwers) to burn them out. The Volkssturm are in action too but reports so far on their fighting abilities have been very derogatory. They appear to be sprinkled in and among the regular troops and any sign of desertion gets them a bullet. Theirs is really an unhappy lot, for prisoners from these divisions tell of the ill-treatment received at the hands of the SS. Their whole training has taken but 1 week and they then find themselves in the forefront of the fighting. They are for the most part very old men, mostly without uniforms or modern weapons. They have to provide their own greatcoats and boots and eating utensils.**

---

* This was the worst weather Holland had suffered in 50 years.
† A flame-thrower mounted on a carrier which could project a flame 100 yards.
** According to Allied estimates, German infantry was being destroyed at the rate of 5–6 division a week. Re-built divisions were appearing in the line with poor equipment and only six weeks of training.

Sunday 26 Nov

The weather has at last cleared up, and a good job too or else we would all have had to don our Mae Wests once more. The RAF took advantage of the weather and were out today in force, bombing and straffing German positions over the Maas and altogether making themselves a nuisance to our opponents. They probably found another German HQ. Both Brit Second Army and American 9th are in a new drive NE of Geilenkirchen and are reaping a rich harvest of Home Guard prisoners – for what they are worth.

Monday 27 Nov

Although the 2 Army are progressing into Germany very nicely, they never actually drove all the Germans back over the Maas in their sector, with the result that three strong pockets of resistance were built up west of the Maas, but today they have erased one of them. Last night their RA turned on the gas with a Victory shoot and then this morning the RAF went in. There was so much destruction when the armour attacked that the tanks just couldn't possibly get through it, but when the infantry finally did get through all the Germans had been killed by the bombardment and there was no fighting.

Tuesday 28 Nov

The Germans have been using their new jet-propelled aircraft against our troops, the most seen being the Messerschmitt 262. This plane can only fly for about ten minutes, but at such a speed that our Spitfires couldn't hope to catch it. It is chiefly used for lightning bomb attacks and they had a go at the Nijmegen bridge. It appears though that owing to its terrific speed its bombing is not accurate. All is still quiet on our front, except for patrols every night across the Maas to bring back a few prisoners. The Germans do likewise.

Wednesday 29 Nov

The Americans are in bitter fighting opposite Cologne and Düsseldorf, for the Germans are resisting like fanatics. The defence works are also exceedingly strong. They have made a few local advances east of Hurtgen. Our life is now identical to our army career in England. We spit and polish and look very smart, all for the benefit of the Dutch. No longer are we in the fight and I'm beginning to wonder when we shall be. Only by careful concentration can we hear the roll of the artillery. Actually we are now some 12 miles behind the line, and our line is almost as quiet as it is here. The sappers are fighting the inundation and have got pumping stations at work with success. Of course nobody knows the country better than the Dutch and their civilian technicians are giving us some very valuable assistance.

Thursday 30 Nov
Gen Patton's men are now holding 9 miles of the R Saar and are only 7½ miles from Saarbrucken itself. It is said that north of the Maas in Amsterdam, Rotterdam and the other principal towns the little children are dying for food, but they still will not commence their railway system. They are very patriotic. The Germans say they can have food if they care to fetch it in their trains from Germany, but I think once the trains got to the Fatherland, it would be guns, not butter they would bring back.

Friday 1 Dec
After we cleared up Walcheren and South Beveland and destroyed Jerry's guns which ruled the Scheldt there still remained the clearing up of the Scheldt itself which was found to be thickly sown with mines. The Navy has been called in and 100 British minesweepers have cleared 70 miles of the Scheldt Estuary in a week. Antwerp can now be used and shipping should be in tomorrow.* This currency is very risky, for Jerry flooded the place with spurious money and already the 1000 and 500 guilder note has been declared useless.

Saturday 2 Dec
Princess Elizabeth today launched the world's biggest battleship. This life is getting us chaps down. We had expected a quick ending to the war and we had built up so high on it ending before Christmas that now we are downhearted as our hopes come crashing down. We take a very dim view of all the sudden regimentalism that has been thrust upon us, after doing so well in Normandy and making a perfect job in Le Havre, when they

* A convoy of 18 ships had reached the port on 28 November. On 1 December more than 10,000 tons of stores were put ashore. Bearing in mind the fact that Rundstedt's Ardennes offensive was only a fortnight away, the opening of the Scheldt was providential.

didn't even mind whether we had a bath or not. It seems ridiculous to learn to slope arms by numbers again. Why can't we get cracking over the Maas? We came out here to finish the war, but I suppose the Generals are afraid of losing their credits if the war finishes too quickly. Leave is the one thing in all the fellows' minds just now, but if they were busy they would never think of it.

Sunday 3 Dec
Bormann, the leader of the German SA, has refused point blank to allow Himmler to take his men for the Gestapo, but Herr Himmler has, in public, said that he will squash Bormann just as he did Göring and Goebbels. Hitler has made no comment on the outburst. This is what we like to hear – disunity amongst the German leaders is better than all the battles we win. Since D Day the Allies have taken ¾ million prisoners.

Monday 4 Dec
The Second British Army with, still in the lead, 3 Br Inf are now blasting Venlo at point-blank range. They've done some very heavy fighting recently and have stuck at it like madmen. They reduce all the German villages as they come to them without offering an ultimatum or terms of any kind. This is so very different to their action in France, but these are German villages, which makes a difference. Montgomery is emphatic, as is Eisenhower to the Americans, about non-fraternisation with the Hun. There must be no speaking to them or giving food or buying souvenirs of any kind. The Hun is prepared to die for the Fatherland and he is prepared to see that you die too.

Tuesday 5 Dec
The highlight of the day is the news of leave for all men who landed on D Day, the first to be home by 1 Jan 45. This has come like a tonic to the men and I at first fell for it head over heels. Then I listened to a few words of wisdom by the Brig, who is no pessimist, but as he said, this leave is going to cause a lot of heartaches at home when the return comes about. I wish it had never been mentioned and that we were to stick it out here to the bitter end. This leave will slow the war down too, which is fatal. For 7 days we shall be extremely happy and then for the next 7 weeks we shall be bemoaning it. Still I couldn't possibly turn it down now that it is commencing. I am as eager as the next.

Wednesday 6 Dec
American troops of the 3rd Army today crossed the R Saar below Saarluis. They used British Bailey pontoon bridges and appear to be very adept now in their erection. This is a very good move on the part of the Yanks and I hope that they can quickly get their armour across and consolidate their gains. RAF out in strength on the marshalling yards of Hamm and Soest.

Thursday 7 Dec
52 (L) Div have completed their commitments on Walcheren and handed over to L of C troops. The Div has now passed under command of 2nd Army. They did a very nasty job well. The general opinion of Walcheren is that the Germans with their superb defences could have held the island for a longer period than they did, but after they had flooded everywhere to a depth (average) of 4'6" they decided it wasn't worth keeping anyway and so retreated northwards to the island of Schouwen. Walcheren and especially Middelburg its capital, is in a bad way. The Dutch people are marooned in their bedrooms and depend entirely on the army for food. The army can only get about the place in DUKWs and these have to travel in twos if one gets into difficulties. These DUKWs are six-wheeled monsters capable of travelling on either land or sea and they are front and rear drive.*

Friday 8 Dec
Jerry found that by inundating Walcheren our activities were cut down considerably and so he is now inundating more land north of the Maas. The civilians are suffering unheard-of hardships for what little food they have is being confiscated by the hungry SS. Br Second Army and the American First still engaged in very heavy fighting and progress is very slow. The Germans have a very good position and are very loathe to leave it. All territory captured now has first to be razed to the ground, but as it is German it doesn't matter.

Saturday 9 Dec
It is said that 300 American prisoners in the sector south of Aachen were lined up in a field by the SS and cruelly mown down by machine-gun fire. The SS then went round the ones that were

---

* The flooding was so bad that the Dorsets tried sinking obsolete tanks into the mud to make firm foundations for strong points.

only wounded and bayoneted them to death. 14 of these American boys shammed death and later made a break of it. 4 of them were killed but the other ten brought back this report. If this is proved to be true then there will be severe repercussions. The Germans say it is only lying English propaganda. I think it will be true alright. This is typically SS.*

Sunday 10 Dec

American First Army still valiantly plugging away have now reached a point only one mile from Duren and one mile from the R Roer and so are able to dominate a line from Duren to Jülich. Allies on German soil are having no small amount of trouble with resistance groups in their rear areas. German snipers from young boys of 12 and 14 years to old women of 60 are being met with. They are very difficult to detect so the only policy, when a town or village is captured with a few inhabitants, is to make everybody stay indoors all the time until the place can be properly policed. A few German communists seem willing to line up with the Allies, but even these are treated suspiciously and their proposals turned down.

Monday 11 Dec

American 7 Army has made a slight advance and captured a place called Hagenau. Close scrutiny at the map will show that the big squeeze is now on, for, from Arnhem to Strasbourg the Allies are now poised on the whole German frontier and in places are over to a depth of 16 miles. Our own front is still very quiet except for patrols. Some of these provide a few talkative prisoners for our Intelligence people. A Sgt of 4 Cdn Armd Div on patrol with his section was confronted by an SS man in the dark. His sten gun jammed up on him and so without much ado he clubbed the German to death with it.

Tuesday 12 Dec

Our desperate enemy in Arnhem has recently had the jitters and has done a little more flooding so that now between Nijmegen and Arnhem 30 square miles are now under water. 2 Cdn Corps can now write home for some more stamps if they think that they

* This may refer to the Malmédy Massacre when 142 prisoners were shot on the orders of Joachim Peiper of the 1st Panzer Division.

are going to get across that lot before this spring. This water never freezes to a depth strong enough to take a Churchill or Sherman.

Wednesday 13 Dec
As First Cdn Army HQ is situated in Breda, 1 Corps in Tilburg and 2 Cdn Corps in the Nijmegen area it has been thought advisable that Army HQ is put between its two Corps, so today we swapped places with Army and we are now situated in the Military Academy, Breda. Breda is a fine old Dutch town, with much history attached to it. There once was a Breda Convention but I've forgotten when and also what it was about. The Military Academy is a fine piece of architecture, built like a castle and surrounded by a moat. The shops are quite empty though and the people, as in Tilburg have a hungry, hang-dog look about them. The Poles, who liberated this town, are very 'well in' here and are still the local heroes. They seem to resent our intrusion and one man of our advance party was thrown in the moat last night. This resulted in two Poles going for a ducking some 3 hours later.

Thursday 14 Dec
There are now 5 Allied Armies on German territory for the American 7th have now made the grade. We are once more introduced to our old friend the V1 and occasionally its partner, the V2. They pass directly over here en route to Antwerp, which has been under ceaseless bombardment from these robots since its liberation. Some of the 'buzz-bombs' have fallen short and exploded in the vicinity. The blast from these missiles is terrific.

Friday 15 Dec
Two German officer cadets were picked up in Breda last night. They were brought to the HQ and spoke very freely. As usual they were on special missions, to disrupt traffic and plant time bombs and in general to let us know that they are still able to hit back. They openly said that we can't possibly win the war now that they have stopped our advance and that very soon we shall be bombarded by bigger and better secret weapons, the saviours of Germany. They fail to understand why we go on fighting and why we don't line up with them against the Russians who are out to domineer Europe. These Nazi fanatics are now thinking over their

master plan in a PW cage. The RAF last night plastered Ijmuiden and the E boat pens with 12,000 lb bombs. If these pens are anything like the ones in Le Havre then they will need direct hits only to make an impression.

Saturday 16 Dec
V1 and V2 in bundles of four every hour pass directly overhead. One broke the ranks and landed in Breda behind the NAAFI. Five civilians were killed and the NAAFI temporarily put out of action. We don't mind so much about the NAAFI for it never was any good, but we are sorry for the civs.

Sunday 17 Dec
We are now planning Op "Pounce", but for security reasons and the fact that this diary is liable even to fall into enemy hands I will make no mention of its object yet. All fronts are very quiet but ours won't be soon when planning is completed. I'm pleased that we are starting something, for I'm sure that we could sit here for the next ten years. The Dutch are beginning to wonder when we will liberate their fellow countrymen north of the Maas, but they realise that we tried very hard with our airborne landing at Arnhem . . . One ex-Dutch officer says that as he knows his country far better than we do, with 40,000 Dutchmen he could get to Amsterdam. I'm afraid that this courageous gentleman underrates our intelligence department. These specialists could tell him much more about Holland that would even surprise him. In any case he knows nothing about modern warfare, and more important, mine warfare. His men wouldn't get ten yards through the extensive German minefields. Our own sappers, who have cleared mines from Normandy to here will have a tough job on, and they must be some of the finest men in the world at this type of work.

Monday 18 Dec
Today we had the biggest surprise for a long time. The Germans opposite the American First Army in the Ardennes have launched a major counter-attack and although there is very little news so far we fear that it is going badly for the Yanks. We know that this sector was very weakly held. I believe only one division was in place. Germans have dropped paratroops in the Bastogne area and also their army has been assisted by fighter planes – proof of this is the fact that they lost 120 today. On our front each day we

get line-crossers. These, usually civilians, cross the Maas under cover of darkness and are picked up by our troops before they get onto our minefields.

Tuesday 19 Dec
German elements are now 20 miles into Belgium and have already captured a few large towns including St. Vith. It looks pretty bad for the Americans. The BBC is very reticent and only gives the barest of news. Our sitreps report that the Germans are subsisting on captured American dumps. The whole plan has been devised by that master-mind Field Marshal von Rundstedt.* The Germans have been conserving their stocks of petrol and used their tanks very sparingly. I notice that some of the old Panzer Divs of Normandy days are taking part in the push. 2 Pz Lehr, 2 Pz Div, 12 and 21 also – the whole push is being made by the 6th Panzer Army. It has been brilliantly planned and executed and so far is meeting with much success. The Americans cannot possibly hope to hold this tidal wave. The Germans claim 20,000 American prisoners so far, but we have made no comment. It is my firm belief that the whole attack is doomed for inevitable failure. We are having more than our quota of V1s. They come over in procession these days.

Wednesday 20 Dec
The advance still goes on and the War Lords openly state that they cannot hold it before Christmas. They are, though, slowing it down. The chief spearhead is pointing towards Liège and it is the German intention to get to Antwerp. The Typhoons accounted for 95 German tanks today and if the weather keeps up there will be a repetition of what happened in Normandy at Avranches. I think that one or two British Divs from 2 Army will shortly be sent to this bulge, perhaps the 53rd Welch for they are closest and resting. This will look bad in the English newspapers. That bitch Mary of Arnhem is crowing over the successful German army and predicts the Allies' total and absolute collapse culminating with another Dunkirk as the main German offensive has not yet begun.

* The attack became known as the "Rundstedt Offensive" to the Allies, though he had played no part in its conception and even disapproved of the plan as being too ambitious. He was obliged to accept the plan when it was presented to him at the end of October, which was endorsed in Hitler's own handwriting with, "NOT TO BE ALTERED".

Mary of Arnhem was actually Gerda Eschenberg. She had lived for years in the U.S. and spoke English almost better than German. She was 18 years old when the war broke out and got a job as a secretary in the English department of the German Broadcasting Company. They broadcast German news in English under the title "Germany Calling". These broadcasts came from Berlin at first, but as the air attacks destroyed the lines to the more western transmitters, they moved into occupied territory, firstly to Luxembourg, then from 1944 to Hilversum in the Netherlands. The programmes were aimed at the British army.

In 1948 Gerda Eschenberg gave interviews to a German newspaper Hoer Zu *in which she explained her motives. She claimed that she wanted to create a better understanding between the two sides in the war by broadcasting items that would show that not everybody in Germany was a Nazi. She wanted an exchange of ideas that would help to build a better world once the war was over. She started her own broadcasts in October, 1944, consisting of B.B.C. reports from London and her own items, using as little as possible of official German programmes. Prisoners of war made use of the station to send messages home, and they even had a P.O.W. working with them for a time. The new programme was called "This is Arnheim Calling", and she presented herself as 'Mary von Arnheim".*

After the capitulation of Germany, she finished up in a prison in Delft with about a thousand Dutch women, where she worked in the laundry. She escaped to Germany in February, 1946.

Thursday 21 Dec
SHAEF declare that Gen Omar Bradley is unable to get to the Belgian bulge to direct operations and that during the Emergency our Field Marshal Montgomery will take full command of the American First Army. Monty is there as are the 51 (H), 53 (W) and the famous 6th Airborne Div. I wouldn't put down on record the opinions of my fellow warriors on the taking under his wing of this American Army by Monty. Our relations with the Americans must always be the best, but this type of fighting is what Sir Bernard got his promotion for – 'slogging', and the British Divs down there are famous at it.*

* Although British troops may have thought this was the right thing to do, the temporary change in command, ordered by Eisenhower, was resented by the American commanders, their troops, and eventually by their people at home.

Friday 22 Dec
As this diary is to be devoted mainly to my activities with 1 Corps, then our own front must needs take priority over even the Belgian Bulge. All Germans on all fronts are now very restless, success has gone to their heads. Line-crossers of last night report a concentration of over 50,000 Nazi troops over the Maas and about 20 miles from here. These soldiers are openly bragging that they will be in Antwerp in a week from now. They are reported to have paratroop elements in their midst. Our aircraft on recce, however, fail to observe any bridging material, but this could be too well camouflaged in the woods. A paratroop landing is expected in the Breda area and so we are all confined to our posts, our Chief Engineer is appointed Garrison Commander, Breda, and we are working overtime getting out Operation Instructions. Our defence is only very weak consisting of the 1 Polish Armoured Div, 4 Cdn Armd Div, 18 Armd Car Regt and a lot of odds and sods. This would be sufficient to contain an attack until reserves were brought up. This is our first setback since we arrived and a few of the chaps are looking down in the mouth. The Dutch people are dead scared that the Germans will come back and I was a little disappointed in Pijnenburg when he said that they would be here for Christmas and he would be shot for collaborating with the British. I must admit it looks bad, for in the bulge the spearhead is still heading for Liège, but close scrutiny of the map shows that Monty's men attacking from the north have already bitten into the German L of C lines. If the Americans attack in the Bastogne area then it is possible to cut off about 10 German crack divs. Bastogne is still heroically defended by an American para div.

Saturday 23 Dec
Further reports from 'line-crossers' tell of huge preparations by the Germans for an attack across the Maas. If he ever does come then I think we've 'had it'. Preparations are made for us to evacuate Breda and set up new headquarters at Baarle Nassau on the Dutch/Belgian frontier. It is very dangerous to go out at night for all bridges and vital points are heavily guarded and these guards are shooting first and asking questions afterwards. Rifle shots and the crackle of stens, brens and revolvers go on all the night long. We are confined to the Garrison.

Sunday 24 Dec
We have managed to scrape up a little more infantry, the Lincs and Wellands, 1 battalion, for the defence of Breda. Jerry sent out active patrols and fighting patrols last night, and early this morning we had the stand to, but he never came. Our 240 Fd Coy caught five Huns on their minefield near the Moerdyk. They were blown to pieces. By now we have sown mines like corn this side of the river and it would cost Jerry dear if he attempted to cross. We too can lay mines and booby traps, although since the invasion we have never had to resort to this type of warfare, being on the advance all the time. Let me see, this *is* the season of Goodwill towards all men I believe. I spent all tonight hatching a most horrible plot for our opponents if they attempt to attack us.

Monday 25 Dec
The cooks made a special effort today and we fed very well indeed. Lots of singing and beer drinking and speech making. If Jerry had attacked about 3pm I'm sure he would have made it easily. We are still confined to Breda with a curfew (slightly relaxed for Christmas) at 2300 hrs. On the pretext of visiting Canadian Army HQ Capt Black and I got a jeep and a pass and went to Tilburg for the evening, he to Cdn Army and I to the Pijnenburgs. We ran the gauntlet for the 15 miles between the two towns. It was rather risky but well worth it. The P's did me very well and I managed to cheer them up for they have got a bad attack of the jitters. We left Tilburg at midnight and Black drove like a madman. We were hailed several times but never stopped, but as we entered Breda and crossed the main bridge I saw for a second a sentry madly waving to us. A split second later I heard his rifle crack out at us. He fired from 10 yards and missed, not much use to stop a German. Quite a good Christmas to say I'm in the middle of a first class war.

Tuesday 26 Dec
The Squareheads made a move this night, after quite a deal of air activity in this sector culminating in the bombing of Gilze airdrome between Tilburg and Breda. He dropped 5 paratroops on the main Tilburg/Breda road, object being to disrupt traffic and perhaps a little road cratering. But everybody was so much on the alert that they were shot as they landed. A truckload of soldiers coming from Tilburg to Breda were ordered to stop by a

party of RAF Regt troops from the airdrome but the driver seeing their blue greatcoats mistook them for Germans and stepped on the gas. The RAF opened fire and killed one soldier and wounded 3 others. It is very risky these days to be out after dark. The Poles are firing at anything that moves.

Wednesday 27 Dec
The OC 240 Field Coy, Maj Woodall, was in today and he says he cannot understand the reason for all the 'flapping' about the Germans coming over the Maas. His company has only seen 5 Germans on the Maas and they were dead ones on their mine-fields. Monty, in command of the Americans is already making good headway against the Bulge. The weather has improved and so we have put the RAF on the advancing Germans. This has tripped them up somewhat and cost them approx 800 vehicles.

Thursday 28 Dec
Both flanks of the German attack into Belgium are now held but the centre, led by that remarkable div 2 Pz Lehr, is still slowly advancing. All is quiet on our front apart from active patrolling. We still expect an attack and our troops are standing to every night. It is now very cold and some German prisoners from their patrols in this sector are found to be suffering from frostbite. Germans on Kapelsche Veer, a small island in the Maas were last night heard singing warlike songs. Our chaps a few hundred yards away joined in.

Friday 29 Dec
We are now taking V1s as a matter of course, until one crashes down in Breda and then we all duck. Frank, I think is in Antwerp, working with the 305 Gen Tpt Coy on the docks. Every time a V1 buzzes over this HQ en route to Antwerp all the chaps shout, "Look out Frank, another b——". British Second Army seems to have come to a standstill, so do the Cdns in the Nijmegen sector. All in all there is very little activity on this front, the main fighting being in Belgium and as aforesaid this attack is doomed for failure. It has now been stopped and, although the Germans have advanced some 35–40 miles the process of annihilation is begin-ning. This will cost Jerry dear for he has been using reserves he can ill afford to lose. And we thought the war would be over by Christmas. I once gambled on the 15th Oct. Blast these Huns. A few more stories of atrocities have filtered through from the north

of Holland, all to be taken down in our little black book ready for the day of retribution.

Saturday 30 Dec
British Second Army recently made a little surprise advance and from a German HQ captured a detachment of Maedchen in Uniform. This is a very interesting capture for these girls in the German Army have a very strange role. One of the girls told the story of how, after her sweetheart was killed she was so distracted and her hatred so intense for the enemy that she volunteered to do anything to help the comrades of her lover. There were many more girls like her and they were formed into a detachment with the title Honour Bright. Their job was right up with the forward troops and they had to willingly give themselves to any German soldier when he wished. These poor misguided maidens act as an excellent weapon for the German Army's fight against VD, of which there is much in the German Army. A doctor is always in attendance and the girls live, eat (and sleep) with the German soldier. This peculiar fanaticism amongst the German people is very hard for the British to understand. Although the Germans have their backs so close to the wall that they can't read the writing on it, there is still no sign of any disunion in their ranks, and they fight like madmen always. Our troops have to fight for every inch of ground.

Sunday 31 Dec
Bastogne which so heroically held out, although encircled, has been relieved and the 101 US Airborne Div who held it are real heroes. The RAF and the AAAF are wreaking havoc on the German tanks and transport, 2 Pz Lehr are being severely mauled by the 53 (W) and two other American Divs. I think that this will be their death knell and the sooner this crack div is wiped out the better. Also two Allied armies on either side of the bulge are starting to advance further into German territory.

Monday 1 Jan
New Year came in with a little surprise for today the GAF came at us in strength. 300 FW 190s and Messerschmitt 109s attacked our airfields and positions on the Maas. It was a day of brilliant sunshine so our RAF was also busy. Out of the 300 attacking planes, 189 were shot down and counted on the ground, for the loss of 45. I hope he comes again then he will get the others shot

down also. They came over this HQ like a swarm of bees at rooftop height. We had only two bombs near here and they fell in fields. The captured pilots ranged from Lance Corporals to Majors, which in itself is a surprising feature. This attack caused another wave of the jitters to sweep through the Dutch population. Of course we mustn't be too hard on them for after all they did suffer a deal under the Nazi rule and if the Germans came back there would be wholesale slaughter amongst those who stayed.

Tuesday 2 Jan
Jerry got a real bullseye on Breda today with a V1 killing quite a number of civilians and a few soldiers; one of our bridges is missing also. The American First and Third Armies operating in the Bulge under the Field Marshal have now taken the initiative and the Germans are fighting heavy defensive battles. This state of tension must be brought to a head in our sector. We can't be on the alert like this all the time, so tomorrow night we have planned to send a strong patrol into enemy territory to find out the real disposition of his troops.

Wednesday 3 Jan
Apart from such activity as was forced upon them by our fighting patrol the enemy has not been particularly energetic during the past week. We are beginning to doubt very strongly the Germans' intention to attack and await the report from the patrol when it returns late tonight. Three men of a German patrol crossed the river north of Geertruidenburg. They were from the 5 Coy 17 Para Regt and their mission was to recce and report movement and to lay 4 Schumines on a footpath in this area, to cut any telephone wires they could find and to determine whether our outposts were Polish or Cdn. Their capture has added to our knowledge the fact of yet another Para regt opposite us.

Thursday 4 Jan
Today we packed up lock, stock and barrel and prepared to move to Baarle Nassau. It looked as though we were really going back for the first time. Then came the surprise. Our patrol returned from over the Maas and reported that they had met very little enemy opposition during the whole of their tour. So, like the army we simply unpacked and stayed where we were. So far as we are concerned the 'flap' is now definitely off.

137

Friday 5 Jan
When the Germans launched their attack on Belgium they thought it would be a good idea to disrupt our divisional dispositions as much as possible and so they persuaded Dutch collaborators to cross the Maas and report to our Army authorities the tales we first heard about the Germans massing for an attack on Antwerp. These stories, the Germans hoped, would make us withdraw our divs from another sector and strengthen this, but their plot was a complete failure for 1 Corps never called for assistance from any other Corps, credit for this falling upon our General, Sir John Crocker.

Saturday 6 Jan
The Americans have launched a big attack on the Bulge and taken a deal of prisoners from 2 SS Pz Div. They have advanced some 6 miles and are now only 3 miles from Rundstedt's lifeline, which is a road leading back into Germany and along which all his supplies must come. The RAF and AAAF are continually bombing and straffing the German troops in the Bulge and it looks as though the German army is once more going to be caught in a 'Falaise Gap'.

Sunday 7 Jan
One thorn in our side on the Maas front is a small island NE of Breda called Kapelsche Veer. This island was never cleared during our grand push, oh so long ago, but our prestige now demands that the German garrison there must be erased. The Huns are quite cocky about their possession and are frequently heard singing, just to let us know that they are there. Then again it is a regular sniper's nest, so we are going to put the Poles on them, and planning is now under way. Our intelligence says there are about 2 Coys in residence totalling some 500 men, they have good fortifications and the island is also well wooded.

Monday 8 Jan
Today we have had the first serious fall of snow and our sappers are manufacturing and operating snowploughs. The Germans in Belgium are running a remarkably successful racket. A whole Brigade, the 150, speaking English with an American accent are equipped with American uniforms and jeeps and are wandering about Belgium unmolested committing acts of sabotage and

138

killing lone American soldiers. This is going to cause complications if not quickly stopped. As spies they are shot.* As a matter of interest here is a list of PW since D Day to 31 Dec in this theatre of operations:-

2 Brit Army	98,350
1 Cdn Army	118,373
9 US Army	60,999
1 US Army	223,563
3 US Army	146,672
7 US & 1 French	158,500
	806,457 Total Nazis captured

Tuesday 9 Jan
The American attempt to encircle the Germans in the Bulge is slowly succeeding and now the Hun has only a 10-mile gap through which to escape. This type of warfare is very much suited to Montgomery and I believe that the Germans wish they had never started on their adventure. The RAF is mercilessly pounding the Nazis for in this snow they show up very well.

Wednesday 10 Jan
German forces in the Ardennes Bulge are beginning to withdraw, the best troops coming out first, i.e. 2 Pz Lehr Div. Only the Wehrmacht are left for the slaughter. British 51 (H) Div and 6 Airborne Troops capture Rocheforet and the road to Houffalize has been cut. Ever since our arrival in Breda the V1 has not once ceased to pester us, although 90% pass over en route to Antwerp, but tomorrow our 84 Gp are out to bomb an important bridge in North Holland over which the buzz-bombs must pass to their launching sites, this information being given to us by a line-crosser, no other than General Jans of the pre-war Dutch Army.

*This was Lt-Col. Otto Skorzeny's 150th Panzer Brigade. More than forty jeep loads of Kommandos got through the lines, and committed acts of sabotage such as cutting telephone wires, destroying radio stations, killing military police on point duty (one even took over and directed a convoy down the wrong road), and waylaying dispatch riders. Eight groups were captured and some were shot as spies, though Skorzeny himself was acquitted of the same charge after the war.

139

Thursday 11 Jan

The RAF must have been successful yesterday for not one V1 passed overhead today. During the recent 'flap' we recruited into our Corps elements of the Dutch resistance personnel. Properly equipped as infantrymen, they took up a portion of the line and were very pleased to do so. They were of course under the watchful eye of one of our Div commanders and he reported much enthusiasm in their ranks. Last night two patrols from one of these Dutch Coys went out on a recce over the Maas, alas, one patrol got out of its area and stumbled into the other patrol, result being that each patrol practically wiped the other out. There will be no Court of Enquiry.

Friday 12 Jan

We plan Op "Horse" in order to kick out the Germans on Kepelsche Veer. The actual assault is to be done by 47 Commando Regt but before they go in, the island is to be subjected to a great deal of bombing and artillery bombardment. This is to last 3 days. The Huns are well dug in so it is to be hoped that the RAF give them a good 'brewing' first. An ingenious idea has been rumbled by us. The Germans were trying to get across the Maas in the 2 Army sector but we had blown their last remaining bridge and they were having to make a strong stand in front of it. Our recce aircraft saw that the Germans had constructed a new frame alongside of the old bridge but as the frame had no flooring to it, it was obviously assumed that the bridge was unfinished. One night our aircraft dropped a flare in the vicinity and was surprised to see that German transport was simply pouring across this bridge, yet on the following day it was again photographed and found to have no decking. What actually was happening was that the Germans were laying the decking at night and getting as much across as possible and then taking it up before dawn. The bridge was systematically bombed and the remaining troops wiped out.

Saturday 13 Jan

The result of our bombing of Kapelsche Veer is that the Germans are pouring reinforcements onto the island. They are determined to make a stand. Our artillery was brought to bear on the moving columns but the results were not observed. The Germans replied to our shelling with a barrage on Geertruidenburg. They appear to have repaired the damaged bridge leading to the

140

launching sites of the V1s for we have been subjected to further attacks today and the rate of fire has increased to 6 to the hour. A Spitfire shot a V1 down immediately above this building and I think it was the biggest explosion I have so far heard in this war. The building literally rocked as though an earthquake had occurred.

Sunday 14 Jan
Montgomery's men have cut the last main escape route for the Germans from the Ardennes. The gap is closed to 9 miles and the American artillery has got 15 miles of artillery for the 'gauntlet' if Jerry chooses to run it.

Monday 15 Jan
It was decided today that Kapelsche Veer had had enough bombing and shelling and was now ripe for the kill. So at dawn this morning the Commandos went in. The initial attack was magnificently done and the river was crossed and a landing effected, then things began to go wrong. The units lost touch with each other when Jerry smashed the wireless. The Germans were found to be very well dug in and our Commandos had not enough ammunition with them to fight it out, so they had to come out. The casualties were only very light, but this is definitely first round to Jerry. It appears that our bombers used only very light bombs so that the craters they caused would not be a hindrance to our tracked vehicles. These bombs were useless.

Tuesday 16 Jan
We don't like to be beaten and yesterday we were, so today we began to plan Op "Elephant". That last Op was "Horse" and the differences between the two Ops is as an Elephant is to a Horse. We are putting the whole of 4 Cdn Armd Div into this Op to take Kapelsche Veer plus 2 AGRAs plus a 4.2 Mortar Platoon plus 84 Group Typhoons and any more infantry the Div commander desires. The whole assault is to be led by none other than 80 Aslt Sqn of 5 Aslt Regt RE. We used to have with us a Lt Baird, a Cdn. He was a perfect gentleman and I think the nicest Cdn I ever met. After his attachment here he was sent to 240 Field Coy RE where he made quite a name for himself as a conscientious and diligent worker. He lost his life today by being a little too conscientious. A minefield had been laid containing

some 200 mines, every mine being plotted so that there could be no mistakes when the time to take them up arrived. However, it was found after the field was laid that 201 mines had been issued from the store and yet only 200 plotted, so Lt Baird and a Sgt went out to find the missing mine. Lt Baird actuated a trip wire accidentally and was blown to pieces, the Sgt was severely injured. This news 'shook' the chaps here for Lt Baird was a very popular man during his stay.*

Wednesday 17 Jan
The Germans in the Ardennes now refer to 'defensive battles', which is quite a change from when they were bragging about cutting through to Antwerp. There is a bitter fight in progress at St Vith and if the Americans capture this town then the German fate is sealed. As it is the gap is now only 6 miles wide, but Jerry is still managing somehow to get his best troops back. One of the finest deeds done by Resistance personnel is now being done in the north of Holland, where the railway strike is crippling the Hun's supply line but at the same time many people are dying of starvation. They would be fed if the railways opened up, but the Dutch were asked by Eisenhower to strike last September and they will not disobey his command.

Thursday 18 Jan
84 Group has commenced its bombing programme of Kapelsche Veer and already the Cdns are in position ready to attack when the word is given, but it will take a few days yet for we can't afford to make any mistakes this time. The Americans had 74,000 casualties in Dec alone and 330,000 since D Day. Our own casualties on a percentage basis are very similar. The heavy snow in the Ardennes is aiding Rundstedt to extricate his troops on one road only as the Americans are struggling across impassable countryside.

Friday 19 Jan
The Russians have launched a major offensive, after a 3-month rest, in which they have 3 Armoured Corps. They steam rollered over Warsaw and 15 miles past it. In the south they are but 15 miles from the German frontier and 60 miles from Breslau. The

---

* Lt Gordon Baird was a 25-year-old from Regina. Some of his fellow Canadian officers felt that he should have been decorated for his bravery.

British Second Army are pushing to the East of Geilenkirchen and are meeting stiff opposition. Our patrols over the Maas have identified 712 Inf Div and 2 Para Div. The incessant snow has cancelled one leave date. All fronts are now active and sparring for an opening.

Saturday 20 Jan
Cracow falls to the Russians, snow falls on Holland, flying bombs fall on Antwerp and 2 Cdn Corps fall on the Germans with success north of Nijmegen. The Belgian Bulge is now only half its original size and much booty and prisoners have been taken recently. As the Americans press this bulge back though, another bulge is appearing in the Strasbourg area and it is up to the French to deal with this.

Sunday 21 Jan
The Russian offensive is gathering impetus and now they are 40 miles past Warsaw and in the south have crossed the German frontier into Silesia. The Americans approach St Vith but are finding it a hard nut to crack. Rundstedt knows that if he loses this place the rest of his forces in the Bulge are lost, so the Hun is fighting like a fanatic. Our Divs on the Corps front are lifting their own minefields, so perhaps we shall see something up here soon. Just now 1 Corps has got the easiest of all sectors and our life in the Military Academy in Breda has taken on a peacetime aspect. We blanco and drill and walk about in a smart military manner. There are no supplies getting through to the civilians though and the shops are still empty. Black Market is the only business. As one walks down the street, especially at night, a host of voices from shop doorways and street corners hail us with 'smoking for money?' Some of the chaps sell cigarettes for as much as 100 for 20 guilders (£2). These civilians then sell them again to the rich for about double that sum. Soap and food are very much in demand also. Most of my cigarettes go when I visit Pijnenburgs for they have many friends who have no cigarettes. I made the acquaintance of one van Gent in Breda. He gave me two lovely boxes of sweets for Mary and also a camera for me. The camera though is a plate model and so not so good for me, but it is a very expensive one, having a Compur Shutter. It is a German Ideal camera.

Monday 22 Jan
Russians only 30 miles from Breslau. The Russian offensive is having a great effect on the Dutch people. They are afraid of the Russians and think that someday they will come right through and fight us. I don't for a minute think on these lines. Poles from our div say that the Russians are worse than the Germans. This still has no effect on me. I hope that the Russians can finish the war the quicker the better. I can't understand why we are so still in the West. Our armies, although all slowly advancing are *not* yet making an all-out effort. There must be some good reason. The Bulge is now only one-third its original size with the Germans still retreating. The RAF destroyed 1100 vehicles yesterday in this fighting.

Tuesday 23 Jan
The RAF has smashed over 2000 vehicles in the Bulge during the past two days. This is because the sun has been out and the German convoys show up so well in the snow. Russians only 15 miles from Breslau, 2 Army advance is speeding up; even in Italy things are beginning to move a little faster. Looks as though the Allies are going in for the kill all round.

Wednesday 24 Jan
In the Ardennes the enemy still falls back to the shelter of the Siegfried Line, helped by the snow which is bogging down the Americans. 6 Panzer Army is getting away and leaving the nondescript divs for the slaughter. The vastness of the Russian offensive in the East and the speed with which it has progressed has materially altered the whole war situation and Germans are very uneasy on this front. Prisoners openly admit that they prefer the British to get to Berlin before the Russians for they are afraid of the reprisals which they seem sure will be meted out. They've asked for such reprisals and it is to be hoped that the Russians take a full and just revenge.

Thursday 25 Jan
Russians 4 miles from Breslau. Our American allies have invented a new shell which is playing havoc amongst our enemies. This shell is of the air-burst type and is rather more than just anti-personnel. Many Huns are being sent to either the hospital or the cemetery every day as a result of its devastating power. One prisoner said that when his battalion was subjected to it three out

of every five Huns failed to get up at the count. The other but smaller German bulge in the Strasbourg sector is being contained for the present and will shortly be eliminated also.

Friday 26 Jan
The Russians are now but 150 miles from Berlin proper, that is half the distance that we are. 4 Cdn Armd Div attacked Kapelsche Veer today and things did not seem to be going as well as we hoped. At 23.30 hrs they were crying for more bridging material. They never did seem to decide how much they would require, but we can't argue with them when they are in the middle of a battle so we got it there OK. Let's hope it does them some good.

Saturday 27 Jan
Russians 100 miles from Berlin and Koenigsberg now completely cut off. This was the startling news of the day. In our POW cages the prisoners are going frantic at this news and some of the big callous SS men are breaking down and crying like children. They are worried about what the Russians will do to their families when they get well into Germany. No doubt these SS men participated in some little atrocities in Russia when they were last there.

Sunday 28 Jan
4 Cdn Armd Div have got their teeth properly into Kapelsche Veer and it looks as though they will take it this time. The sappers got them onto the island OK and they are steadily wiping it out. A V1 landed in Breda and killed 16 civilians, one also in Tilburg killed a party of the Pioneer Corps.

Monday 29 Jan
Russians 80 miles from Berlin and still going strong. Field Marshal Sir Bernard Montgomery has relinquished his command of the American forces in the Ardennes and it is now announced that the Belgian Bulge is completely wiped out. General Omar Bradley has resumed command of his troops. This is another feather in Monty's cap. There is now such a strong force of both British and American AA in the Antwerp area that out of 100 V1s 73 are shot down. Prisoners tell us that at the launching sites only 3 in every 5 V1s get away. The launching is a most dangerous operation and many men are burned. Russian prisoners are forced to launch these bombs – or starve. This of course is against all the rules of modern warfare, but Jerry waives such trivialities.

Tuesday 30 Jan
Russians 75 miles from Berlin and still going strong. 4 Cdn Armd
Div captured Kapelsche Veer and have inflicted 475 casualties
killed, their losses being 349. It has been a tough fight for the Cdns
for it was found that the defence works were very substantial. We
used Crocodiles (flame throwers) to finally winkle the German
garrison out.* Prisoners from KV will not believe what our men
tell them about the Russian advances, but say that it is just British
propaganda. The Germans still in St Nazaire are in a peculiar
position. The French Maquis is handling the job and it is just a
matter of time before the Hun packs in. He has destroyed all elec-
tricity stations and water supply plants, blown up the docks and
harbour installations. He thought the French were going to take
the place but the French are leaving him to stew in his own juice.
A German plane delivers the mail every evening to the trapped
garrison – news from home must be very sickening just now.

Wednesday 31 Jan
The Russians by cutting off Koenigsberg have trapped a full
German army part of which has been trying to escape by sea but
the Red Air Force has already sunk two troop ships. It is looking
very sick for the Germans on the Eastern Front just now. The
Russians are also only 30 miles from Frankfurt on Oder.

Thursday 1 Feb
Russians now only 60 miles from Berlin, but the German radio
says that this is not true and that the Russians are actually only
40 miles from the capital. In the West the enemy is on the defensive everywhere. American 1st and 3rd Armies are over the
German frontier on a 30 mile front. Once more we are experiencing the same exhilarating feeling we had when the Germans
collapsed in Normandy. Soon I think 1 Corps also will be in
Germany. I hope that the end is very near and that the Germans
will be unable to reorganise their forces in the East. They are a
very surprising race and even when it looks as though they are
hopelessly beaten they seem to pull something out of the bag.

---

* The 80 Assault Sqn. R.E. landed the Canadians aboard "Buffaloes"
which had to be prised through the ice using crowbars and sledge-
hammers. It was so bitterly cold that men who fell into the river had to
be evacuated as casualties. The Engineers improvised means of crossing
the ditches with, for example, rescue rafts from the "Buffaloes".

Friday 2 Feb
The French forces under General Leclerc dealt very effectively with the bulge that occurred in the Strasbourg area. They have completely wiped it out and inflicted 22,000 casualties on the 35,000 Germans in this bulge. The French are excellent troops and have some Moroccans fighting with them in this mountainous district.* Soon the French will have another full army in the field. The trials of the 'collaborateurs' in Paris are very interesting. The judges are showing no mercy whatsoever and the guillotine is busier now than it has been since the days of Robespierre.

Saturday 3 Feb
The Germans trapped in East Prussia now only hold $1/10$th of the province and this, not for long. The Russians are now only 45 miles from Berlin. It will be interesting to see what they will do when they reach the Oder. This river will take some bridging. I wish we could lend them a bit of Bailey. They don't use Bailey and I think it is the only bridging that would do to keep up the speed of the advance. They are, however, excellent at rafting and ferrying so perhaps they will make do this way. The Oder is only frozen at the sides; this makes rafting awkward. The Americans dropped 2,500 tons of bombs on Berlin during daylight today, then the planes carried on to have a look at the Russian front. Our troops have crossed the Maas north east of Breda and south-east of Nijmegen. This is 2 Cdn Corps. 15 (S) Div are concentrating in the Tilburg area and it appears that 51 (H) are coming up too. This means that 30 Corps are coming into First Cdn Army and that a big push is in the offing.

Sunday 4 Feb
The First French Army has captured Colmar and taken 2,500 prisoners in 24 hours. The Russians are now less than 40 miles from Berlin and have reached the Oder on a 40-mile front. Letters taken from German prisoners on Kapelsche Veer tell of the state of things within the Reich. One wife wrote to her soldier husband – their home was in Wiesbaden, it had suffered from the bombing, her nerves were in shreds, she had no food, she didn't expect to

* They were Goumiers – Moroccan tribesmen from the Atlas Mountains serving with the regular French African Infantry. They were well suited to mountain fighting.

147

live much longer as another raid would just about finish her off. She longed for the war to end as did everybody else in their town – the town was only a shell anyway. It must be remembered though that this very same woman and thousands like her cheered their soldiers to victory in 1940 and their demands for parcels from occupied countries cleaned these places out. Unconditional surrender is their only alternative to sudden death by bombing, we must not weaken for a minute. Himmler has appealed to his enemies to lay off this indiscriminate bombing as the GAF in 1940 never subjected London and other big cities to such infernos. That was only because they couldn't. Unconditional surrender is the only alternative.

Monday 5 Feb
Marshal Zhukov's forces have reached the River Oder at several points and have reached a point 35 miles from Berlin. We are now presented with the spectacle of the ordinary people of Germany being subjected to those very miseries to which they have callously subjected many millions of people in the occupied countries. It is easy, at a distance, to support plans for the hard treatment of a defeated Germany. I wonder if it will be as easy to carry them out when we are on German soil. With their post-1918 years to guide them the Germans may show considerable guile in their efforts to win our sympathy but we must not let sympathy deflect our minds. The Soviet writer Ilya Ehrenburg wrote "The crackling of flames in German towns sounds like music in my ears. I am happy that I lived to see this day."

Tuesday 6 Feb
Brisk patrolling on our front indicates that something is afoot, 4 Cdn Armd Div were patrolling in strength as were the Poles also. The Germans used all their strategic reserves in their Ardennes offensive and their casualties amounted to 220,000, half of them prisoners. This makes 1 million since D Day.

Wednesday 7 Feb
A prisoner recently captured on our front seemed to have a good sense of humour. He says that Hitler has ordered, that owing to the severe shortage of manpower, the pregnancy period for a woman is now to be cut to six months instead of the usual nine previously allowed. He says that many of the German soldiers opposite our artillery have been digging their slit trenches so deep

148

that they are being accused of desertion. In Southern Alsace American troops have seized the western end of the Rhine crossing at Neuf Breisach. They had to use rubber boats and scaling ladders in the final assault.

Thursday 8 Feb
The Big Three are meeting in the Black Sea area. Complete agreement has been reached for the joint military operations in the final phase of the war against Germany. They are discussing the problems involved in the setting up of a secure peace, including plans for the occupation and control of Germany. The Russians have broken into Elbing a most important port in East Prussia.

Friday 9 Feb
A huge force of Lancasters were out today bombing positions immediately in front of 2 Cdn Corps and 30 Corps (now in First Cdn Army) and we are expecting a big attack to follow up this bombing.* Setorious has been tipping the Second Brit to make an attack soon. It will come as a surprise when he finds the Cdn Army open up first.

Saturday 10 Feb
Brit and Cdn troops of 1 Cdn Army launched a new assault into Germany on a 5 mile front south east of Nijmegen, between the Maas and the Rhine. The front was later broadened to 6 miles and forward units were 6 miles into German territory. They have broken through the first Siegfried Line defences and are well into the Reichswald Forest. 2000 prisoners have already been taken and 12 frontier villages have been cleared. We in 1 Corps are feeling a little out of it. Our sector is quite quiet, but I think I prefer to clear out the west coast of Holland to carrying on into Germany.

Sunday 11 Feb
Cdn Army attack is going very well and Scottish troops (15 (S) Div) have captured the German town of Cleves. They are now fighting in the second of the Siegfried defence belts SE of Nijmegen. They are also more than halfway through the Reichswald Forest. Monty says that the battle is going nicely but

---

* This was the preliminary to Operation Veritable, an attack through the Reichswald Forest.

the mud was not helping things. I ought to have said yesterday, that when this new attack began the rain simply poured down. Still our Met people should know about this in advance.*

Monday 12 Feb
The mud is slowing the Canadians on the left flank and the battle is likely to be stiffer from now on. Strong resistance is being offered by a German parachute div brought from Alsace. Marshal Konev's Russian forces have crossed the Oder on a 100 mile front and got nearly one third of the way to Dresden in Saxony.

With Operation Veritable in full swing, the diary inexplicably ends. My late mother said that there was a second volume which covered the push into Germany and the end of the war. I do not recall ever seeing this, though I have my father's photographs of the area around Iserlohn, where he finished his military service with the army of occupation in 1946.

---

* Another factor was that, since the plan had been made, a thaw had set in which turned the forest rides into quagmires. In Cleves itself, the attack came to a halt because the streets were blocked with craters and rubble. Horrocks had requested that Cleves be bombed with incendiaries, but high explosives had been used.

Appendix 1

General Crerar "has sent a personal message to the Cdns not to retaliate on the Germans for their atrocity of murdering 20 Cdn prisoners."

I was not able to find the actual text of Crerar's message in the War Diaries, but in the Log and Summary of Events of my father's unit, it simply records: "13 July Personal message to all troops from C in C." (Op. cit. 13 July, 1944) This was not much to go on, but fortunately the full text of the message appeared in many newspapers at a later date. I quote from *The Times*, 3 August, 1944: "General Crerar in his message to the troops declared that there could be no doubt of the deep anger which would rise in the heart and mind of every Canadian. 'The universal and natural determination of Canadian soldiers to avenge the death of our comrades must not under any circumstances take the form of any retaliation in kind. The commission of atrocities will be left as the bestial prerogative of Hitler's Germans. Instead Canadian anger must be converted into a steel hard determination to destroy the enemy in battle, to hit harder, to advance faster, and above all, never to stop fighting and fighting hard while life remains. If any reminder is needed concerning the issues we are fighting for, and the evil forces we are fighting against, this has surely been provided.'" Some sketchy details were given in the same report: "Ottawa August 2nd. Mr. Mackenzie King, the Prime Minister, disclosed in the House of Commons today that 19 Canadian prisoners of war had been murdered by the German forces in Normandy . . . The P.M. said that in the early days of the invasion of Europe, General Eisenhower received a report that some Canadian soldiers had been shot after capture by the enemy. He established a court of inquiry to investigate the report. The court found that one Canadian officer and 18 Other Ranks who had been taken prisoner were murdered by the 12th SS

151

Reconnaissance Battalion of the 12th Panzer Division, under the direction of their officer. These Canadians had the status of prisoners of war and were entitled to protection, and the manner of their death was a clear violation of international law."

The *Daily Herald* claimed that the murders had taken place near Pavie, Calvados, on 8 June, north of the Caen–Bayeux road which the Canadians were battling to cross. Thirteen had been shot in one group, and the others in small groups. The bodies were buried by the Allies, later exhumed and complete autopsies carried out. There was proof of the events from French civilians.

The victims of the massacre were largely members of 'A' Company of the Royal Winnipeg Rifles. On 8 June, under the command of Major F. Hodge, they were holding a defensive position to the west of Putot-en-Bessin. At about 9.30 a.m. the 2nd Battalion SS, commanded by Oberst Bernhardt Siebken, attacked the Winnipegs' position at Putot. This battalion was part of the 26th Panzer Grenadier Regiment commanded by Colonel Mohnke. The battle raged all morning and the Winnipegs came under pressure from artillery, mortars and tanks, so that by 1.30 p.m. they were completely surrounded by the enemy with little ammunition left (the situation was such that the Canadians could get no ammunition forward), and the majority of their automatic weapons had been knocked out. An attempt was made therefore to withdraw the survivors under cover of smoke, with stretcher bearers operating under fire. Very few got back to Battalion Headquarters; three of the four companies had been almost completely wiped out. On 9 June the surviving "Little Black Devils" dug in for defence, had their first hot food since landing, and filled their water bottles for the first time in France.

The prisoners from 'A' Company were turned over to the 12th SS Recce Battalion whose battle Headquarters were at the Château d'Audrieu, near Pavie. Here, according to a SHAEF Report, "it has been established that 19 of these prisoners were ... on the order apparently of an officer, murdered in cold blood by organized firing squads. It is believed that on another occasion that day seven more suffered the same fate." (SHAEF Report of Inquiry into the Shooting of Allied P.O.W.s by 12 SS Panzer Division in Normandy, 7–12 June 1944: FO 371/50977)

The events of that day were the subject of a Court of Inquiry held at the Château d'Audrieu between 11 and 16 July, 1944, presided over by General R.W. Barker. The findings must have prompted Crerar's message on the 13th. A number of civilian witnesses gave their testimonies, and one, Monique Livry-Level (now Corblet de Fallerans) later wrote her account in her autobiography. She was the daughter of the château owners. Her father, Philippe Livry-Level, had escaped to Britain and joined the R.A.F., and regularly flew sorties over France (including his own home). At the time of the Inquiry, Monique accepted from the Intelligence Service a reconnaissance mission in the zone still occupied by the Germans south of the Odon. She was arrested by the SS between Baron and Every. Initially condemned to death as a spy, the sentence was commuted to deportation, and she spent the remainder of the war being shunted between concentration camps including Ravensbruck and Torgau. She returned to her home after liberation. Ironically, she left for her mission straight from delivering her testimony to the Court of Inquiry. She was 20 years old. I had the good fortune to meet this brave woman, purely by chance, on my 1995 visit to Normandy.

On 8 June, at about noon, the 12th SS Recce Battalion of the 12th SS Panzer Division (Hitler Jugend), under the command of Major Bremer, set up a Command Post at the rear of the château. The unit consisted of three officers and about fifty other ranks. The family remained in the château. The Germans asked them why they had not left, for the château would in all likelihood be destroyed in the coming fight. One told the witness Beatrice Delafon that Canadians "with big knives" had been captured one kilometre from the château, and it was implied that they should remain hidden, for the Allies might kill them.

There was much activity throughout the day and Monique and her cousin Beatrice sat reading in the garden at the rear of the château, to observe the comings and goings. Towards 2.00 p.m., three Canadian prisoners were taken to the headquarters tent and interviewed, and then marched across the park towards the woods. At one point one prisoner hesitated and was struck by one of the three SS guards. Shortly after they entered the woods a series of shots rang out and the three guards returned alone.

The second incident happened shortly after when Monique witnessed from her bedroom window four prisoners being marched towards the woods. She left her room at this point, but her cousin watched and listened from the attic, and later reported the shootings to Monique. From this point, the alarmed witnesses made the kitchen their base where, Monique writes in her autobiography, to calm themselves, they recited the burial service in Latin.

At one point an officer demanded civilian clothes, blackened his face with burnt cork and then, she thought, went towards the village with a flame thrower. He returned the clothes two or three hours later. At about 5.00 p.m. a German soldier came to the kitchen. "He took a round box of cigarettes from his pocket and said: 'Good English cigarettes. I took them from the prisoners and we kif-kif them' (indicating a throat cutting gesture). Then he said, 'No, not like that; it was with my revolver' and at this point he took his revolver from his holster and put it back into his holster saying; 'it was I who killed them.'" (Testimony of Monique Livry-Level, Proceedings of a Court of Inquiry held at Château d'Audrieu, July 11–16, 1944: WO 219/5045 p. 443)

The third incident was far more serious and I think forms the real basis for the claim in my father's diary. Between 4.30 and 5.00 p.m. a group of thirteen prisoners was led towards the hen house in the south-west corner of the park. Leon Leseigneur, the farmer of the château, saw them from a sunken road as he passed by. Some were standing, others reclining, guarded by a group of German officers and NCOs. On his way back from moving the bull from its place in the pasture, he heard rifle, pistol and machine-gun shots from a distance of about forty metres. An employee, Eugène Buchart was with him and supported his testimony.

At 5.00 p.m. Raymond Lanoue, the son of the gardener, went towards the hen house to retrieve two pigs which had escaped. In his statement to the Inquiry he describes how he found the pigs snuffling among the corpses of the Canadians. Two German soldiers stood by, one with a revolver. He called for the pigs – "Schwein de retour" – and a German guard replied, "Viens ici; viens ici; Tommies kaput" and gesturing with his revolver the length of the hedge shouted, "Tommy, tat-tat-tat-tat." He then drove the pigs back to the boy, who noticed that their snouts were covered in blood. The gardener went to investigate the incident when his son reported it to him. The bodies were being searched by two German soldiers, so he returned at 10.30 p.m. after the Germans had pulled out. Six of the Canadians had no boots, none had their equipment, a few helmets were scattered about. Some held photographs and a couple had prayer beads.

Between 6.30 and 9.40 p.m., there was much shelling and machine-gunning in the village and the vicinity of the château. During this time, the Germans withdrew, but remained in the immediate area. The village itself was taken by the 1st Battalion, the Dorset Regiment. On 9 June Monique Livry-Level went to the village to report the murders to the British. She accompanied Captain J.F. Neil of the RAMC to find the bodies but, as she records in her autobiography, as there were only the two of them, it was impossible to find those who had been shot in the woods. "Instead, I showed him the prisoners who were shot near the hen house. It was a frightful sight, thirteen young men shot in the nape of the neck with a bullet, lying side by side in the green grass, their empty eyes popping out of their sockets. An enormous hole was beside them probably to bury them but time was lacking and the crime could not be concealed." (Monique Corblet de Fallerans, *Voyage Nocturne au Bout du Parc – d'Audrieu à Ravensbruck*, Editions Heimdal Bayeux, 1992, pp. 68–69) This is the only reference I have found to a hole being dug, as claimed by my father. There is no other evidence to suggest that the Canadians dug their own graves. Rumour was rife in those tense situations.

The military position was very confused at this point. The Dorset Regiment's War Diary reports counter-attacks and they left Audrieu that same day. Consequently, Captain Neil did not submit a report of his findings until 12 or 13 June.

The family left the château for the next few days while fierce fighting raged in the area. On 14 June, the Hallamshire Battalion of the York and Lancaster Regiment (49th Division) moved into Audrieu. The War Diary records: "June 15 Château at south end of village occupied by 'B' Company. Contained many bodies of British and German troops, while in the garden was discovered by the Bn. Padre the corpses of 14 O.R.s of the Regina Rifles who had been stood up against a bank and shot through the head in cold blood." (WO 171/1304 15 July 1944) The mention of 14 Regina Rifles, which was perpetuated in Jacques Henry's *La Normandie en Flammes* and in Brigadier T. Hart Dyke's *Normandy to Arnhem* initially caused some small difficulty in my research, but as the Winnipegs and Reginas (both prairie regiments) were brigaded together, it was an understandable error at the time. Coincidentally, while conducting my research, I met veterans of the Battalion after the funeral of Brigadier Hart Dyke in June, 1995. Ex-Lieutenant Raymond Langdale described moving through the grounds of the château with a small group of men and finding Canadian documents and paybooks scattered on the ground, and then the grim discovery of the corpses. Some had no boots, their battledresses were open, and each had about three shots in the head.

The battalion had with it a Canadian officer, Captain Lloyd Sneath. He had joined the Winnipegs in 1940 and transferred to the Sheffield battalion under the CANLOAN scheme. He recognized some of the dead. He later gave his evidence to the Court of Inquiry. Approaching the château on 14 June, he picked up the "Advance Book" of Major Hodge. 250 yards further on, he found Hodge's Record of Service, personal letters, snapshots, and a Nominal Roll of 'A' Company, 1st Battalion Royal Winnipeg Rifles along with some paybooks. The papers were trampled, but still legible. He knew some of the men. He reported the finds to the second-in-command of the Winnipegs and learned that 'A' Company had "disappeared" since their action at Putot. He went to the château the next morning with the padre to bury the dead. There they saw the bodies close to a fairly thick hedge running east to west from the hen house. "They were in an irregular line a few feet out from the hedgerow, generally speaking parallel with each other . . . Each man had been wounded in the head. In some cases the top of the head had been lifted completely off." (Op. cit., p. 414) He immediately recognized Sgt Louis Chartrand. He knew him very well, he was of Indian extraction and very easy to identify.

Padre Thomas also gave his evidence to the Court. He and the C.O. Major Lockwood (with a sten gun nearby, for the wood was not yet cleared of Germans) gathered up the identity discs and documents. One or two held photographs of their wives or girlfriends. ". . . it looked to me as if one or two men had taken out these photographs to have one last look." (Op. cit., p. 416) He decided not to arrange the burial at this point (15 June) for he was convinced that they had been shot as prisoners of war and an investigation would have to be made. But the battalion was moved five days later, and so then arrangements were made. Not until two weeks after the murders were the bodies buried.

Brigadier Hart Dyke recorded in his memoirs: "Audrieu was altogether an unsavoury area with large numbers of dead cattle lying in the fields, the woods were eerie and dense and there was always the fear of mines, booby-traps and snipers up the trees. The château itself had obviously been the scene of a desperate fight earlier on as dead bodies littered the stairs. We were glad when we moved forward from Audrieu." (*Normandy to Arnhem*, published by the 4th Battalion Yorkshire Volunteers, Sheffield, 1991, p. 10)

The thirteen murdered Winnipegs were identified as W.C.

Adams, E. Bishoff, L. Chartrand, S.J. Cresswell, A.A. Fagnan, R.J. Harper, H.A. Labrecque, J.L. Lychowich, R. Mutch, H. Rodgers, S. Slywchuk and two brothers, F.V. and G.E. Meakin. All had multiple wounds, mainly to the head. They ranged in age from 18 to 26 years. On 22 June R.S.M. Hopps of the 185 Field Regiment, R.A. was sent with a burial party to locate and bury the three bodies from the first incident. They found Major F. Hodge (with severe wounds to the face and shoulder), L. Cpl. A.R. Fuller and Rfn. F. Smith (the latter belonged to the Queen's Own Rifles of Canada). German cartridges lay nearby. On the same occasion, the party came across the bodies of the second group consisting of Rfn. D.S. Gold, Rfn. J.D. McIntosh and Rfn. W.D. Thomas. None of them had arms or equipment or paybooks, and some were without boots. All are now buried in the Canadian Military Cemetery at Bény-sur-Mer.

On 26 June Sgt. G. Minards of the 289 Field Park Company R.E. was sent with a party to bury British dead from the battle. They found a group of seven bodies (five Canadian and two British) in a decomposed state, hidden by undergrowth. Four had identity discs and two had other documents with which to identify them. Some of their other documents were found along with documents belonging to the murdered Canadians. It is probable that they were murdered too on 8 June, but as only one of the group had actually been seen to be captured, the case for murder of P.O.W.s is not so strong.

The inquest could not find conclusively which German officers gave the orders to shoot the prisoners. Monique was unable to recognize the officers among the photographs shown at the Inquiry, though it was clear that the commander wore the decoration of a Knight of the Order of the Iron Cross. The SHAEF Report of May 1945 named certain officers as being present and ordering or cooperating in the murders, and claimed that the C.O.'s driver and motorcycle dispatch riders probably carried out the killings. In addition to the 12th SS Recce Battalion, there was the Signals Platoon of the H.Q. Company at the château that day. No court case was ever brought against these accused men though in 1949, at Aurich in Germany, the Allies instituted proceedings against Bernhardt Siebken, C.O. of the 2nd Battalion SS which had engaged the Winnipegs at Putot. He was hanged. But Lt.-Col. Lockie Fulton, C.O. of the only surviving Winnipeg company at Putot said that Siebken had treated his prisoners well. He was not really responsible. He paid for the others.

The 12th SS Panzer Division (Hitler Jugend) had a reputation among fellow German troops which earned them the nickname, the "Murder Division". The SHAEF Report claimed that this division had the idea, given by the officers, that the British did not take prisoners, and therefore, by implication, they should do the same. It was also nicknamed the "Baby Division" because most were teenage volunteers – 65% were aged 18 years. Only 3% were over the age of 25 years. They had gone through Nazi political indoctrination and so fought fanatically for their cause. In his war crimes trial in 1945 Major-General Kurt Meyer was accused of inciting the 12th SS Division to murder prisoners in the so-called Secret Order: "4th Order: The SS troops shall take no prisoners. Prisoners are to be executed after having been interrogated. The SS soldiers shall not give themselves up and must commit suicide if there is no other choice left." (Record of Proceedings of the Trial by Canadian Military Court of Kurt Meyer at Aurich, Germany 10–28 Dec, 1945, Vol. III: (WO 235/599) In his appeal against the death sentence, he claimed never to have issued such an order, and that he could not be held responsible for actions committed by soldiers under such an enormous strain. He also said that the atrocities (of which there were so many in Normandy), were not committed by young soldiers. He was convinced that those responsible had been brutalized by five long years of war, especially against the Soviets on the Eastern Front. Curiously, Hart Dyke records in his memoirs that civilians in Audrieu claimed that Russian soldiers in the German army had carried out the murders.

One French historian, M. Georges Bernage, has put forward a theory that the Audrieu murders were in fact reprisals for a British atrocity. His researches suggest that on the morning of 8 June a group of nine German officers and N.C.O.s were captured near to Brouay and Christot by two reconnaissance patrols of a British armoured regiment. As the British were in a highly dangerous situation, and short of space in their light reconnaissance vehicles, they were faced with a dilemma. They could not let such important prisoners go; neither could they load them into the tiny vehicles. The two senior officers (one a colonel) were attached to the turrets of two vehicles; the remainder were shot. One officer in this last group, though severely wounded, survived and was later recovered by the 2nd Battalion, 26th Regiment, and reported the incident to Siebken. Meanwhile, the British reconnaissance patrols were spotted near Le Mesnil-Patry and fired upon by the anti-tank guns of the 26th Regiment. One German officer was mortally wounded, the second, unscathed, was saved. Profoundly shocked by what had happened to his comrades, he incited the Waffen SS in this particular sector to seek revenge. The news of the murders rapidly spread.

Georges Bernage suggests that this surviving officer asked that allied prisoners should be entrusted to his division, whose right wing was to be found effectively in the proximity of Audrieu. This would explain how Canadians captured at Putot finished up at Audrieu, which was in fact a dead end on the left wing of the Hitler Jugend front, and certainly not en route to the rear. Certainly the patrols of the British regiment in question were in the right area at that time, and the War Diary indeed claims that a German colonel and other officers were captured. On their return to British lines, the diarist reports that they were ambushed and lost their vehicles. Only four O.R.s made it back. Did the Winnipegs pay for the sins of their comrades, just as Siebken was to pay for others?

One other incident is worth noting. Monique Livry-Level testified to the Court of Inquiry that on the evening of 8 June, when the Germans withdrew, they left behind a badly wounded 19-year-old SS soldier. They took care of him, but he was anxious that they should not be found by the British, otherwise they would all be shot. "I told him that the English did not shoot their prisoners and he did not believe me. He told me a story which I did not understand very well. The story was that his Colonel had been taken prisoner by the English and wounded by the British and he later escaped from the British." (Op. cit. p. 425) This testimony seems to suggest that the execution of the German officers was known about by the Germans in this sector from the afternoon of 8 June. At the same time, on his person, they found a written order: "The English shoot their prisoners, so as a reprisal, we shoot ours. If you are captured you will be executed so fight to the death. You have nothing to lose." (*Voyage Nocturne* Op. cit. p. 67)

In the heat of battle, it was difficult for the Germans to surrender. Alexander McKee quotes a veteran of the 6th Armoured Regiment who said: "They come forward aligned down the muzzles of enemy guns, and a single shot fired by one man can cause thousand of others to follow suit . . . it was organised confusion . . . men going forward to surrender were shot down, and this could easily be, and most probably was,

159

misinterpreted as deliberate ruthlessness on the part of the Canadians." (Op. cit. p. 86) At the same time, the Germans were up against it, suffering huge casualties. "Can you imagine a young officer asking, 'What about the prisoners, sir?' You can imagine the reply: 'To hell with the prisoners, do what you like with them.' So it gets handed down to, perhaps an NCO, and he is not too happy, or feels the pangs of revenge, or wants to show his determination for the Fatherland, and decides to erase the problem the easiest way." (Ibid. p. 94)

In the course of my research, I found many stories of atrocities on both sides. There were many rumours and stories in circulation, as witness my father's very next claim in his diary. I cannot pass judgement, but enough to say, that when I stood at the spot in the orchard at Audrieu in the general area where the murders took place, and later at the graves of those Canadian boys, I felt a profound sadness at the waste of young lives and the loss of innocence that drove men to this.

Appendix 2

Accidental bombing incidents like those of 8 and 14 August were all too common. The date of the first major incident referred to by my father was actually 8 August and it was a part of Operation Totalise that went wrong.

The first phase of the operation involved the R.A.F. dropping 4,500 tons of bombs in a daring night time raid, commencing at 11.00 p.m, on 7 August. Half of the one thousand bombers did not drop their bombs because smoke and dust had obscured the markers, so wisely turned for home. The raid was a success and on 9 August *The Times* was able to report: "Even while the bombing was still in progress and the troops were moving over the start line General Crerar could send a message to Air Chief Marshal Harris stating that in timing and accuracy the operation was completely successful and hoping that the army would continue the battle as well as the bombers had begun it."

The ground attack of the second phase was due to go in at 2.00 p.m. on the 8th. As a preliminary, 678 Flying Fortresses of the USAAF were to drop 2,000 tons of bombs on enemy targets, from 12.30 to 2.00 p.m. (This timing was in fact a mistake – such bombing was not entirely necessary, but it meant that the armour could not move until after 2.00 p.m., and so everything was slowed down.) Three of the four areas were accurately bombed, but the fourth area could not be safely identified, and only one bomber bombed it. 492 planes had actually dropped their bombs. But later waves of bombers became disorganized by heavy anti-aircraft fire, dust, smoke, (there was no wind to blow it away), and even enemy fighters, so tragic mistakes were made. The Official American History says: "Short bombing within friendly lines resulted from gross errors on the part of two twelve-plane groups. In one case, faulty identification of target by the lead bombardier led him to drop near Caen, although fortunately,

161

some other bombardiers of the formation cautiously refrained from dropping with him. In the second instance, a badly hit lead bomber salvoed short and the rest of the formation followed in regular routine." (From W.F. Craven and J.L Cate, *The Army Air Forces in World War II*, Vol 3, University of Chicago Press, Chicago, 1951, p. 251)

90,000 lbs. of fragmentation bombs fell on Canadians, British and Poles. Among those hit in these two incidents were the 1st Hussars (6th Canadian Armoured Regiment) who lost eighteen men (eight of them killed), the North Shore Regiment (100 casualties), and the main H.Q. of the 3rd Canadian Infantry Division, killing ten and wounding twenty, mainly in the Signals Office, most notably wounding the C.O. of 3rd Division, Major-General Keller. In the factory complex at Colombelles, a Royal Canadian Artillery unit lost thirty-three casualties. Petrol and ammunition dumps went up, guns were knocked out and vehicles destroyed. Various totals have been given for the human casualties. The accepted figure is sixty-three killed and 250 wounded, but a more recent publication gives a higher toll – eighty-six killed, 376 wounded, with seven guns and eighty-three vehicles destroyed. (R.T. Bickers, *Friendly Fire*, Leo Cooper, London, 1994)

Members of the 1st Polish Division, 4th Canadian Armoured Division and 8th Canadian Infantry Brigade who were victims of the incident in the Cormelles area to the south of Caen, were waiting for the go ahead for Totalise. The War Diary of the North Shore Regiment reports that the regiment had been ordered forward when "we were bombed by our own aircraft (Fortresses) and suffered heavy casualties, 23 O.R.s killed, 73 O.R.s wounded and two officers wounded." (WO 179/2947, 8 August, 1944) The Chaudières were also hit: "On leaving the city of Caen, a squadron of heavy American bombers bombed in error the southern outskirts of the city and caused considerable damage. From our unit, Lieut. A. Miller, 2nd-in-command of the anti-tank platoon was killed instantly. Major J.L Taschereau and Captain Pierre Labrecque were wounded and had to be evacuated. After a delay caused by obstacles, debris from houses blocking the roads, the Battalion continued its advance." (War Diary, Op. cit. 8 August, 1944)

While this was happening, my father was witnessing helpless Canadians being bombed in a cement factory by one box of Flying Fortresses (twelve planes not 300!) The 240 Field Company R.E. was nearby. The War Diary reports: "Colombelles Factory bombed by USA planes." (WO 171/1600, 8 August, 1944) The unit at the receiving end was the 2nd Canadian Survey Regiment R.C.A. Their Diary was obviously written up a little later and refers to a photograph: "This picture appeared in the London *Daily Mirror* for 9 Aug. 44. It is captioned "This is War Along the Straight Road to Falaise". The picture has been identified by the C.O. of this unit and the O.C. 'P' Bty as showing 'P' Bty BHQ being bombed by our own planes about 1300 hrs. 8 Aug, 44. The buildings occupied by the above mentioned battery of this unit have been identified from the photograph. The narrative accompanying the picture is quite wrong from a study of the details. The picture was taken with the photographer facing CAEN, not facing FALAISE as witness the ambulances returning from the front and the jeeps travelling towards the front on the opposite side of the road. If this was an enemy position being bombed there would not be a great concentration of "soft-skinned" vehicles so close to the front line. The men crouching in the centre foreground are not infantry waiting to go into action, as they have no web or equipment. Eye witnesses say this is a picture of Canadian troops being bombed by allied bombers. The casualties sustained by 2 Cdn Survey Regt. RCA as a result of this bombing, are: 3 officers wounded, and 13 O.R.s killed and 17 wounded." (WO 179/3077, 8 August, 1944) I have seen this photograph in a number of books and museums, and it is always captioned as the bombing of enemy targets on the road to Falaise. However, a copy of it was presented to me by Lt. Walter Horne, ex–Duke of Wellington's Regiment, as a picture of the incident at Colombelles.

During the course of my researches I corresponded with and met a number of veterans who were involved in both of these or other similar incidents. Rfn Les Wagar of the Queen's Own Rifles of Canada saw both attacks go in: "As the attack began, 3rd Division was on the move forward from our beach holiday to join in the battle as it developed. Getting through Caen was a logistical nightmare. I had gone ahead with Recce to plot our gathering-areas to the south of Caen in preparation for the arrival of the fragments of the Division as they came through the bottleneck. Thus I was on the long slope looking back down at Caen as the American Superforts started coming in from England on their way down the road to Falaise. Fleet after fleet were coming across, to the east of Caen, each a great solid wedge of planes in close order, each wedge having one navigator in its lead plane to direct its coordinates and bomb run. We watched and cheered as they went over. But suddenly one wedge veered off its southward course, and turned westward toward Caen. Consternation rippled along the slopes: I saw the yellow smoke of "friendly" identification flares start up from a half-dozen points along the slope. No effect. The wedge came on. We watched in horror as the whole wedge, as if one plane, released its bombs, and watched them fall like elongated sheets of rain, and watched the centre of Caen boil up in a long, erupting line of dust, debris, and smoke from their explosions. Then another wedge, seeing the bomb-run of the first, veered back from its course towards Falaise, and made its bombing run from south to north across the city . . . We cursed the Americans for their mindless "following the leader", for that was what it appeared to be. We cursed the lack of ground-to-air communications. Most of all we just cursed in impotent frustration."

Pte Frank Rowlands of the Pioneer Corps experienced that feeling of powerlessness. He was in a sunken road near Colombelles queuing for his lunch, when there was a sudden huge bang, followed by pandemonium. Everyone scattered and took cover where they could. His major was killed. Eventually, the dazed unit was evacuated, but all Frank's kit was lost. The only item that was eventually recovered by a salvage party was his rifle. Later, he was put on a charge – he had not noticed that a shell splinter had damaged his rifle.

G.M. Baxter was based in Mondeville with the Air Observation Post, working with Canadian guns. He saw a R.A.F. Mosquito go up which bravely flew rings around the leader in an attempt to stop the bombing, but unfortunately the Canadian guns had already been badly hit. "I understand that later the Leader said he had mistaken the target. This was supposed to be at Falaise, many miles away." S.D. Robinson was with the Royal Signals attached to 143 Field Regiment R.A. His unit was based in Giberville, the same as my father. "As I recall we were situated against a railway embankment. Looking back there was this ruined factory and I made a sketch of it – this was August 7th, 1944. Later we witnessed the bombing by the Flying Fortresses." He kindly let me have a copy of his sketch.

The 7th Battalion The Duke of Wellington's Regiment was in Cagny. The War Diary reports: "Heavy attack by American heavies on enemy positions opposite Cdns. At 1330 hrs. one flight of Flying Fortresses passed over Bn. area flying North West and by mistake bombed a Canadian medium battery and amn. dump

164

very near Caen. Many casualties." (WO 171/1288 8 August 1944) Nearby, the Armoured Divisions were moving up to commence their attack. Spr John O'Neill of 87 Assault Squadron R.E. was driving his AVRE when trouble developed in the gearbox, a cracked casting, so steering was nigh impossible. The crew had to stop and send for a transporter. In the early afternoon, he was resting by the side of his tank, when the ground shook and he could see trees disappearing from the nearby hills. "The Fortresses flew from the direction of the German lines over us. Why they came that way I will never now . . . all hell broke loose. A Polish Division had heavy losses. An Auster plane tried to warn the leader. Our ammo dump was blown up. It went on exploding for days. It was the only one this side of the river. If the Germans had decided to counter-attack, we'd have had nothing to stop them with."

Jan Victor Derych was with the artillery of the 1st Polish Armoured Division south of Caen. He remembers that day well: "It was a terrifying half-hour as the Flying Fortresses were dropping the bombs. One could see the hatches opening and the bombs falling directly overhead. Nearly all of them fell in the next field where our Canadian friends were. The unit was decimated and had to be reorganized. But one of the most heroic memories I have was of the little plane (flying jeep we called them) flying under the Fortresses, I assume trying to stop them or making them aware of the carnage. At that time there was no direct link between ground and the aircraft. There were various reasons circulated (as they usually are and at mysterious speeds). Some said that the bomber mistook some smoke (there were many burning buildings at any time) and let go with his load, others followed. Another story was that the Germans became aware (somehow) of the approaching waves of bombers as they were crossing the Channel and one of their planes dropped bombs behind our infantry lines but close to the back up forces, that is, our artillery position. Yes, our fear, terror was very great since we could do nothing, move nowhere, too late to dig. There was a saying among us – 'when German bombers come, the Allies duck; when British bombers are overhead, the Germans duck; but when Americans raid, both sides duck'."

While all this was going on, Lt Walter Horne sheltered in a ditch with others of the Duke of Wellington's. Canadian survivors made their way back through the Dukes' lines with their clothes scorched and smouldering. L.Cpl Jack Armitage of the 7th

Battalion Duke of Wellington's Regiment was with the Regimental Aid Post. "I was laid outside my slit trench as I knew the USAAF was coming over to continue the bombing. Sure enough they started coming in south of us over the Orne Canal and coming out at a different height over us and on their way back to England. After many boxes, suddenly this box appeared flying in the way that all the others had come out. The next thing I heard was a sound like a rushing train. I immediately rolled into my slit trench thinking that the Luftwaffe had got over the top of the bombers and was dropping bombs through them. As it turned out it was this box of US bombers that were dropping their bombs in the wrong place. (As I understand it each box is controlled by a master bomber who says when the box drops its bombs.) As far as I know their first ones landed on this Canadian medium battery, then they hit an ammunition dump . . . We were told to stand by to go and work on the casualties . . . but we never did as the 146 Field Ambulance was nearer . . . The story was that the Canadian battery was wiped out."

One man who had to help deal with the casualties that day was Sgt. Lloyd Taylor. He was with the 21st Field Dressing Station of the 2nd Canadian Division, based in caves at Fleury-sur-Orne. "That's where we really earned our meagre pay. I was ordered to pick up General Keller who was badly wounded a short distance away. Pte. Carl O'Callaghan was with me when we arrived at the scene of devastation. The infantry, engineers etc., were all in the ditches. An ammunition dump in an old barn was spewing its deadly contents all over the area. Tracers were quite visible – knee-high. General Keller and a wounded priest were in a battered farmhouse 100 – 150 yards away. Although quite scared, we decided to put our training to good use. We crawled on our stomachs to the farmhouse and bandaged up Keller and the priest. Once in the ambulance, the priest wanted one of us to go back and pick up his Bible. Guess what we told him. The casualties came to our Field Dressing Station by the dozens – Brits, Canadians and Poles. Most of them were in shock – trembling and in fear. We kept them warm, a shot of brandy, a cigarette, thence back to the Casualty Clearing Station."

On 14 August, my father writes about the 51st Highland Division suffering casualties as a result of accidental bombing by the R.A.F. This incident did not just affect the 51st Highland Division.

The second phase of Operation Tractable involved the bombing of Quesnay Wood and Potigny by almost 800 heavy bombers and forty-two Mosquitoes. Between them, they dropped 3,723 tons of bombs, beginning at 2.00 p.m. and taking one and three quarter hours to do it. The first waves hit their targets accurately, but unfortunately, seventy-seven Lancasters (including forty-four flown by 6 Group, Royal Canadian Air Force) dropped their bombs short, from two to five miles inside Allied lines. The mistake cut a swathe of destruction through the Canadian, Polish and British ranks. The Canadians alone lost 112 killed, 367 wounded, 265 vehicles and thirty guns. The Polish Armoured Division lost forty-two killed and fifty-one missing.

One basic problem was that there was no direct communication between ground and air. A message from a unit under fire would pass from Brigade H.Q. to Divisional H.Q., to Corps H.Q., to Army H.Q., then on to the Senior Air Staff Officer and on to Bomber Command, and thus out to bombers which were flying at 250 m.p.h. A further compounding factor was that ground troops used yellow smoke canisters to identify themselves as friendly to their own aircraft. As they came under the bombardment, they sent up yellow smoke in a desperate effort to warn their blundering allies. But on that particular day, due to a breakdown in communications between Army and R.A.F., the target shells being lobbed into enemy lines were also yellow. The pilots assumed that they were seeing Pathfinders' target indicators, and the more yellow smoke they saw, the more they bombed.

Again, brave attempts were made by pilots of the Air Observation Post to turn the bombers away by flying around them in their tiny Auster planes. One of these pilots, Eversley Belfield wrote: "I climbed at full throttle and with very great difficulty (I had forgotten how it worked) fired off a red Very cartridge at 2,000 feet and another at 4,000 feet. At about 6,000 feet I was just below a large formation and twisted and turned to attract their attention . . . I am certain that none of this third wave bombed our own forces as I was in the midst of a stream of planes . . . I could plainly see the large bombs in the open bay." (Quoted in *Maple Leaf Route: Falaise* by Terry Copp and Robert Vogel, Maple Leaf Route, Alma, Ontario, 1983, p. 114) Harris said afterwards, however, that the Auster planes simply added to the confusion.

The bombs fell in the rear of the lines, thus the infantry units moving up to the front and the artillery were hardest hit. The 7th Canadian Infantry Brigade War Diary records: "Op. Tallulah commenced today with Bomber Command of the R.A.F. leading off. Due to the close proximity of the Regina Rifles to the target which was Quesnay Wood, they were told to keep well underground and were issued with absorbent cotton in order to plug their ears. The first wave of bombers swept over the target and scored direct hits, but the next waves somehow got off the track and dropped their eggs to the left and rear of Bde H.Q. in our own gun areas. Wave after wave did the same thing – Bde H.Q. was fairly well ringed with bombs. Frantic calls were put in to higher formation to try and correct the bombers' error. Capt. G. Eckenfelder, Sigs Offr, and Sgt Biscoe, Int. Sgt, stood out in the open with a beacon lamp signalling that we were friendly. Yellow smoke was thrown out in all directions but to no avail. Finally around 1545 hrs. when the situation seemed desperate our flying Artillery OPs sized up the situation and at great risk to themselves soared in to the blue and guided the last wave of bombers to the target. As you can imagine everyone around the Bde H.Q. heaved a sigh of relief, but it was close while it lasted. Without a shadow of doubt if it hadn't been for the magnificent work of the flying OPs things would have been more serious for us than they were." (WO 179/2879, 14 August, 1944)

One of the worst-hit regiments in the 2nd Canadian Division was the South Saskatchewan Regiment with sixty-five casualties. Sgt Les Robertson had moved forward with 'B' Company. "Somewhere around midday word came we were going to withdraw about one mile so that the Air Force could cover the whole area in front by saturation bombing. Then the order came that we would maintain our position because if the whole brigade fell back, the Germans may try to break out. (I suppose no one told the Air Force.) Then the plotter planes came over with their flares which they dropped in front of our position and the first wave of bombers dropped everything within the marked area. Then the next plotter planes came, but they dropped their flares behind us. The next wave of bombers proceeded to bomb the entire area. It is difficult to describe the confusion. The tank crews were endeavouring to signal by dropping smoke bombs out of their turrets but the coloured smoke only added to the mess by mixing with the dust and earth flying in the air. In the meantime, I was still standing in my hole untouched, but keeping an eye on the next wave of bombers and when I saw one open the bomb bay doors and let his load go in direct line with my position, I took off running down hill about 25 yards and jumped into a bomb crater from the previous drop on the theory 'lightning never hits the same place twice'. After this last set of bombs went off, I headed further down the hill, but noticed a movement in some bushes to one side. Instinct or training made me pounce on top – it was a very young German sniper left behind. I took him prisoner with his own rifle as I had no tunic or weapons left. I reported to the Regimental H.Q. and then accompanied the colonel on his carrier back to our Company position. One other sergeant, Thompson, survived. He thought that I had been blown to bits as he had found parts of my tunic and paybook. Sgt Thompson and I divided the Company – what was left, there were no officers – and we proceeded to Falaise. Later, a sniper got Thompson right through the heart."

In the case of the 13th Canadian Field Regiment, "Bombs fell within the gun area of the 22nd Bty near the H.Q.s of the 22nd and 78th Btys resulting in the death of Bdr. McDougall and Gnr. Ford and the loss of five essential vehicles. All guns remained in action. A total of twelve 1,000 lb bombs dropped in the area in addition to many anti-personnel bombs. Heavier loads fell in the areas of other units adjacent to this regiment and the obvious destruction was quite a blow to the morale of the troops." (War Diary: WO 179/3051, 14 August, 1944) On 14 August Gunner R.G. Haine of the 4th Light Anti-Aircraft Regiment was manning a 40mm Bofors gun, as defence for the 25 pounders of the 13th Field Regiment. "As the second wave went over, for some unknown reason an ammunition dump one third of a mile to the west of us exploded and live shells came as far as our position. After that many planes started bombing us. We had smoke pots to signal the planes but our Sgt didn't know how to light it, which likely saved our lives. The other Bofors crew (300 yards to the N.N.E. of our position) lit their 'pot' and at once were bombed, killing several of the crew. The third wave bombed everywhere and killed many Polish soldiers and destroyed all the tanks near us except for three. After the raid I helped some Polish officers bury several (17 or 18) of their dead. As no one was firing at them, many bombers came down to a very low level. It was possible to see the pilot of one bomber looking down at us. I ran into the open field near our gun, removed my shirt and waved it over my head. The pilot appeared to waggle the wings and then the bomb doors opened and they released the whole bomb load. I plugged my ears and raised my chest off the earth (after a fast dive) and was not injured at all. The tail gunner also fired a long burst which missed me by a good 30 or 40 feet. About that time someone in a Miles Auster plane went up and met the last flight and led them to the correct target area. I did hear his name but cannot recall it now but I understand he was decorated for his very brave act. We managed to move forward only about 15 minutes late, but there were many soldiers and much equipment destroyed and left on the field. Our next position was beside a small wood on the way to Falaise. As we tried to dig our gun pit a Spitfire swooped low and shot up our ammo truck. It went up in a ball of fire and smoke and at once three American Thunderbolt dive bombers attacked the area. Our major arrived and ordered us to shoot down any planes attacking. Thank God they were the last. In 1966, my brother died and I found most of the letters I'd written home, except for the one I'd written August 14th '44. In it I had told my parents 'I may get killed in this war but remember I have lived through this day, the worst ever.' I guess some censor had thought that was too revealing and had destroyed it."

In their frustration and desperation, some Canadian gun crews did fire on their fellows and one bomber was shot down by Canadian anti-aircraft fire. Dick Raymond and his team of gunners were dug in with their four Vickers machine guns to the east of Quesnay Wood, watching the R.A.F. bombers come over from the north and to their right. "The first bombs were on target hitting the wood, but succeeding planes 'walked' their bombs further back north over the Canadian and Polish front lines into the rear areas. Some planes circled around after dropping their bombs. One plane in particular flew low over our gun position and the rear gunner fired on us. I could see the gunner's face over the barrels of his gun. I was so God damn angry I did not have the presence of mind to turn the Vickers to an anti-aircraft mount and shoot back. A Vickers had a range of 4500 yards and I think I could have hit him."

On this day, the 12th Canadian Field Regiment was based around a quarry at Hautmesnil. Signaller Fred Rogers, with the 16th Battery, had just come off switchboard duty at 2.00 p.m. and went to stand on the loading quay by the railway to get a better view of the waves of bombers overhead. As he watched, he saw the bomb doors open in planes just a thousand feet above him, and the bombs come tumbling out. Thus began over one hour's bombing. Men cowering in their trenches asking incredulously, 'How can they mistake us?' and 'Why can't we stop them?' After each stick was dropped, the air was filled with flying debris and the ammunition from dumps and vehicles exploded in every direction. The Regimental War Diary records: "This day will long be remembered by the regiment for it was a disastrous one . . . the regimental area was systematically bombed . . . Yellow smoke, flags, air OP interference had no effect. 16th Battery badly hit, then 11th. Nearly all vehicles and trailers of the 16th Battery were destroyed and most guns damaged. 11 killed, 1 missing, 1 died of wounds and 53 wounded . . . M.O. did fine work during and after . . . He worked in a tunnel and but for this cover loss of life might have been greater". But the agony was not yet over for the 12th Field Regiment. "August 15th 16th Battery remained all day in quarry to refit . . . recovering from a bad state of nerves. Whole regiment was badly shaken and morale definitely hit . . . moved near Olendon. Greeted there by two Spitfires which attacked own troops very close by and started fires. Later on several Mustangs attacked vehicles on road near position and destroyed a 60 cwt. of the 43rd Battery. No one hurt as the crew hit the ditch in time. Personnel very nervous now and dive for slit trenches at sound of a plane particularly if Allied". (WO 179/3050, 14–15 August, 1944)

Another signaller, attached to the 4th Canadian Armoured Division, who remembers the helplessness of the situation is James C. Johnston. "Our signals truck was situated just behind a line of medium 5.5 artillery guns of which seven gun emplacements and crews were plastered severely. Many of the men were streaming past our position obviously in shock. I could look up and see the bombs as they left the bomb bays, they were extremely low. My earphones were alive with futile requests to stop the bombing. We were only a divisional H.Q. so we did not have direct communication with the bombers. Their orders were directed from Army H.Q. We did manage to send up an artillery spotter aircraft flying under the bomber stream flapping his wings apparently to no avail. I'll never forget those cries for help, especially when you are helpless to do anything about it. Later in civilian life, I met one of the actual bomber crew of that raid at a party in Vancouver. A rare twist of fate."

The support company of the Régiment de la Chaudière was caught at St Aignan de Cresmesnil. The Chaudières' historians wrote: "The bombardment lasted from 1400 to 1530 hours. Not one vehicle, not one gun, not one tank was spared. Capt. J.L.A. Giguère was killed as well as many soldiers. Of two others hit by a bomb, one could find nothing to identify them. Two sections of the carrier platoon were wiped out. A truck containing the records of the Regiment was destroyed by fire. It was carnage. Many became insane". (Ross and Gauvain Op. cit., pp. 48–49)

Spr Percival J. Carter of the 18th Field Company, Royal Canadian Engineers, was also at St Aignan that day. As the bombing began he headed for some tanks hidden in bushes 400 yards away. "A sergeant yelled to me and the others to stay in our positions but I paid not a bit of attention. Myself and a comrade crossed to those bushes with huge bomb fragments going by us like freight trains, and we saw all the Sherman tanks there with their hatches open and the crews sitting on the ground on the other side". As they dived under the closest tank, he kicked over the silver tea service belonging to the C.O. of this armoured unit. He was to pay for this with a severe telling off. They sheltered for the best part of two hours, and when they returned to their unit, they were subjected to another reprimand for failing to remain in their positions. "There were huge craters that the bombs had made. One of them hit the section truck that I travelled in and my extra clothing was in that truck. It was a twisted burnt-up pile of metal lying at the bottom of a huge crater. To have remained there would have meant being blown to pieces instantly. Many of my comrades had been killed in it and others wounded. Others did not show up for several days afterwards."

It was in this area that the 51st Highland Division was to be found, and among others, the Argyll and Sutherland Highlanders were hit that day. The Division suffered more casualties from Allied fire in the following days. On the 15th Allied bombers hit the gun lines behind the 154th Brigade H.Q. and thirteen trucks of the 1st Gordons were lost. On 16 August the 5th Seaforths were dashing along the main road to Lisieux, one mile short of the River Vie, "And then the usual trouble began. The Camerons had actually had to stop advancing because Spitfires had knocked out every wireless vehicle on their establishment. Now Lightnings began to strafe the Seaforth and kept doing it time and again". (J.B. Salmond, *The History of the 51st Highland Division, 1939–45*, Wm Blackwood & Sons Ltd, Edinburgh, 1953, p. 166) On the 18th Typhoons kept strafing behind their lines and even Rennie, the Divisional General had a narrow escape. Brigade Major John Thornton of the Seaforths was killed.

From 17 August onwards, the War Diary of the 51st Division contains an intense, sometimes bitter correspondence from Major-General Rennie to H.Q. of 1st Corps on the subject of air cooperation, to the effect that there were so many incidents of his men being straffed by Spitfires and Typhoons, that it might become necessary for him to withdraw his troops from threatened areas. On 19 August he supported his claims with a summary for 18 August alone: "Number of reported incidents – 40; officers killed – 2; officers wounded – 9; O.R.s killed – 3; O.R.s wounded – 37" (WO 171/528, 19 August, 1944)

But Salmond, the 51st Division's historian concludes: "Nevertheless, let the civilian reader remember that, had the Division not had the air superiority they were enjoying, strafings by hostile planes would certainly have been very much worse". (Op. cit. p. 166) And, "The very speed of the Division's forward movement does much to explain the tragic results of the R.A.F. and American Air Force bombing of our troops". (Ibid, p. 169) When it comes down to it, this is what my father is saying too.

Mistakes like these were hard to swallow. In spite of what had happened, 'Bomber' Harris refused to accept ground-to-air communications between his Air Force and ground troops. Some Canadians saw this as "territorial imperatives being more important than the common good" (Rfn. Les Wagar). An interesting illustration of the dilemma of keeping up morale and trust and accepting that mistakes could happen is the story of Lt. Gen. G. Simonds (G.O.C. 2nd Canadian Corps) who was returning in a jeep to Corps Main H.Q. with his A.D.C. on that fateful day. "The bombs had started to fall. I [A.D.C.] remarked that 'here we go again' and Gen. Simonds who was sitting in the front seat next to his driver Jarvis (I was in the rear seat) spun around on me and said, 'It is only enemy mortars or counter-battery [fire].' I will always remember Jarvis in the rear-view mirror raise his eyebrows in a most revealing gesture. I think Gen. Simonds also knew that the R.A.F. had made a similar mistake to the U.S.A.F. but he just could not, for the moment, accept it and all its grave possible consequences. Then, on looking up, there could be no mistake. The bombers were very low . . . and we could see the bomb-bay doors open and the bombs drop out – looking as though they were going to land right on the jeep . . . The bombs landed on both sides of the road. I would swear one or two landed less than 200 yards from our jeep. But there was never any suggestion by Gen. Simonds that we got for the ditch. We just went straight on to Corps H.Q. . . . ." (Letter, Marshal Stearns to the author, 5 October 1981, quoted in R. Roy, *1944 The Canadians in Normandy*, Macmillan, Ottawa, 1984, p. 264)

There was an enquiry on Harris' orders. The guilty crews were punished – some squadron and flight commanders lost their commands and were put on ordinary crew duties, along with two Pathfinder crews. All the crews involved were suspended from operations within 30 miles of the forward line, pending reassessment after further operational experience.

At the end of it all, Crerar in his communication to Harris, maintained that the heavy bombing had been necessary, in the main accurate, and had contributed in large part to the success of the operation. But Bradley slowed the sealing of the Falaise Gap to avoid the unintentional shooting of allies and to prevent what Eisenhower called 'a calamitous battle between friends'.

Bibliography

Georges Bernage, *Les Plages du Débarquement*, Editions Heimdal, Bayeux, 1983.

Georges Bernage, *Le Terrible 8 Juin 1944*, in 39/45 Magazine No. 68, Editions Heimdal, Bayeux, 1992.

Richard Townshend Bickers, *Friendly Fire*, Leo Cooper, London, 1994.

George Blake, *Mountain and Flood. The History of the 52nd (Lowland) Division, 1939 – 1946*, Jackson Son & Co., Glasgow, 1950.

Omar Bradley, *A Soldier's Story*, Holt, Rinehart & Winston, 1951.

Canada's Battle in Normandy, the last of three booklets known collectively as The Canadian Army at War. The Department of National Defence, Ottawa, 1946.

John D. Cantwell, *The Second World War; A Guide to Documents in the Public Record Office*, HMSO, London, 1993.

Terry Copp and Robert Vogel, *Maple Leaf Route: Falaise*, Maple Leaf Route, Alma, Ontario, 1983.

Monique Corblet de Fallerans, *Voyage Nocturne au Bout du Parc – d'Audrieu à Ravensbruck*, Editions Heimdal, Bayeux, 1992.

W.F. Craven and J.L. Cate, *The Army Air Forces in World War Two*, Vol. III, University of Chicago Press, Chicago, 1951.

Ken Ford, *Assault Crossing: The River Seine*, 1944 David and Charles, Newton Abbot, 1988.

Lt.-Gen. R.N. Gale, *With the 6th Airborne Division in Normandy*, Sampson Low, Marston & Co. Ltd., London, 1948.

Brig. T. Hart Dyke, *Normandy to Arnhem*, published by the 4th Battalion, the Yorkshire Volunteers, Sheffield, 1991.

Max Hastings, *Overlord and the Battle for Normandy*, Michael Joseph, 1984.

Jacques Henry, *La Normandie en Flammes. Normands et Canadiens dans la Bataille de 1944*, Editions Charles Corlet, 1984.

Henry Maule, *Caen*, David and Charles, Newton Abbot, 1988.

Alexander McKee, *Caen: Anvil of Victory*, Pan Books Ltd., London, 1972.

Maj.-Gen. R.P. Pakenham-Walsh, *The History of the Corps of Royal Engineers, Vol. IX, 1938–1948*, The Institution of Royal Engineers, Chatham, 1958.

Majors A. Ross and M. Gauvin, *Le Geste du Régiment de la Chaudière*, Rotterdam, 1945.

Reginald Roy, *1944, The Canadians in Normandy*, Canadian War Museum Historical Publication No. 19, Macmillan of Canada, Ottawa, 1984.

J.B. Salmond, *The History of the 51st Highland Division, 1939–1945*, Wm. Blackwood & Sons Ltd, Edinburgh, 1953.

Col. C.P. Stacey, *La Campagne de la Victoire*, the Official History of the Canadian Army in the Second World War, Vol. III. Published by the Ministry of National Defence, Ottawa, 1960.

Col. C.P. Stacey, *The Canadian Army, 1939–1945*, an Official Historical Summary, Ministry of National Defence, Ottawa, 1948.

Luce Triboulet, *Pour Retrouver Mons Fils à Caen*, published privately, 1960.

Warren Tute, *D Day*, Sidgwick & Jackson, London, 1974.

Chester Wilmot, *The Struggle for Europe*, Collins, London, 1952.

The Yorkshire Pud, a newsletter published by the Education Section of the Duke of Wellington Regiment, 1944–1945.

Index

179

180

181